AF324726

THE HEALTHY CUISINART

AIR FRYER OVEN

COOKBOOK

1000-DAY DELICIOUS LOW-CARB AND FAT-BURNING RECIPES FOR YOU AND YOUR FAMILY

BEVERLY RYAN

CONTENTS

INTRODUCTION

How Does the Cuisinart Air Fryer Oven Work?

Air fryer is an oven feature that works like a countertop air fryer. Inside an air fryer oven, super-heated air circulates around the food to provide crispy, golden results without all the oil that deep-frying requires.

Air fryer ovens eliminate the need for another countertop appliance by putting the same technology right in your oven.

The Benefits of The Cuisinart Air Fryer Oven

During the last few years, these appliances are arguably the most respected and trendy thing that is happening in the kitchen. In comparison to other ways of frying, there are several benefits to use an air fryer.

1.   The Cuisinart Air Fryer Oven May Stimulate Weight Loss

Higher intakes of fried foods are closely related to a higher risk of obesity. It is because deep-fried foods happen to be rich in fat and calories. Swapping from deep-fried foods to air-fried foods and reducing the daily consumption of unsanitary oils will help to minimize weight loss.

2.   The Cuisinart Air fryer Oven May Be More Stable Than Deep Fryers

Heating a huge container full of scalding oil requires deep-frying foods. This could pose a danger to defense. There is no chance of wasting, splashing, or inadvertently hitting hot oil as air fryers get hot. People should carefully use frying machines and follow guidelines to ensure safety.

3.   The Cuisinart Air fryer Oven May Save Lots of Space

You could enjoy this advantage if you have a tiny kitchen, or live in a dorm room or communal housing. These systems are often the size of a coffee maker. They do not take up too much space on the fridge, and it is typically easy to store or pass about.

4.   The Quality of Electricity

These fryers are more powerful than an oven, and they are not going to heat up your home.

Using Tips for the Cuisinart Air Fryer Oven

1.   Use the Right Cookware

A perforated pan (sometimes called a perforated crisper tray) allows air to circulate under and around your food for even crisping. If you don't have one, you can use an oven-safe cooling rack. Line the bottom of your oven with aluminum foil or put a baking sheet under the rack below to catch any drips or crumbs.

2.   Spread Out the Food

If you overload your pan to the point where food is piled up or touching, the exteriors won't brown as well, and it will steam instead of bake or air-fry. Instead, spread it in an even layer with plenty of room between each piece for air to circulate.

3.   Cut Your Food Wisely

There's a reason why french fries are in long sticks — it's because this shape maximizes their surface, providing plenty of exterior for browning. Cut foods into long sticks or small, bite-sized pieces. If you are cooking something like tofu, try tearing it into pieces instead of slicing. The craggy shape will encourage the jagged edges to get crisp and brown.

4.   Prepare Food Properly

The drier your food is before it goes into the oven, the better. Also, spraying it lightly with cooking spray or brushing or tossing with a neutral oil (like vegetable or grapeseed oil) will help encourage browning and crisping and will give a hint of that deep-fried taste we love.

5.   Be Sure to Flip

Air fryer recipes usually recommend flipping the food halfway through cooking. This helps it cook and brown evenly. Don't omit this step in the instructions if you're using a convection or regular oven. After you flip, spritzing the other side with more cooking spray will also ensure both sides are equally crisp.

6.   Know How to Adjust a Recipe

Air fryers cook hotter and faster than a conventional oven, so be aware that your recipe might take a few minutes longer. Start checking it for doneness at the time indicated in the recipe, and if it doesn't look browned enough, check every three minutes until it's golden brown and delicious!

In terms of temperature, air fryer recipes usually recommend a temperature of 20 to 25 degrees lower than you'd cook that type of food in a conventional oven, but the same holds true for convection ovens, so you can likely use the same temperature setting in an air fryer recipe for your convection oven. Cooking in a regular oven or toaster oven without a convection fan? Crank up the temperature by 25 degrees and make sure the oven is fully preheated before putting the food inside.

Tips on Cleaning Your Cuisinart Air Fryer Oven

Along with the racks, your oven interior, exterior, and trays also require regular cleaning if the appliance is used frequently. Here are a few oven cleaning tips that you might find helpful:

- Remove and soak panel knobs in water and dish soap; this allows for thorough cleaning of both, the panel and knobs
- Use the self-cleaning option if your oven has one
- Stubborn grime on interior walls of your oven can be loosened and removed by spraying with a warm solution of 3 part water to 1 part vinegar; wipe with a damp cloth thereafter
- Fill the tray with hot soapy water and scrub when the water cools down
- Clean the inner glass door with a layer of water and baking soda paste (leave to sit for 15 minutes); wipe with a soft, damp cloth to remove traces of the baking soda
- Clean the exteriors glass with vinegar and water, or an eco-friendly glass cleaning product
- Be extremely careful with oven cleaner on natural stone surfaces, it makes it very easy to damage
- Even after utilizing commercial products with instructions, there's still a chance to damage your oven. Be careful spraying oven cleaner on stainless steel surfaces.

BREAKFAST

Nutty Whole Wheat Muffins

Servings: 8

Cooking Time: 11 Minutes

Ingredients:

- ½ cup whole-wheat flour, plus 2 tablespoons
- ¼ cup oat bran
- 2 tablespoons flaxseed meal
- ¼ cup brown sugar
- ½ teaspoon baking soda
- ½ teaspoon baking powder
- ¼ teaspoon salt
- ½ teaspoon cinnamon
- ½ cup buttermilk
- 2 tablespoons melted butter
- 1 egg
- ½ teaspoon pure vanilla extract
- ½ cup grated carrots
- ¼ cup chopped pecans
- ¼ cup chopped walnuts
- 1 tablespoon pumpkin seeds
- 1 tablespoon sunflower seeds
- 16 foil muffin cups, paper liners removed
- cooking spray

Directions:

1. Preheat the toaster oven to 330°F.

2. In a large bowl, stir together the flour, bran, flaxseed meal, sugar, baking soda, baking powder, salt, and cinnamon.

3. In a medium bowl, beat together the buttermilk, butter, egg, and vanilla. Pour into flour mixture and stir just until dry ingredients moisten. Do not beat.

4. Gently stir in carrots, nuts, and seeds.

5. Double up the foil cups so you have 8 total and spray with cooking spray.

6. Place 4 foil cups in air fryer oven and divide half the batter among them.

7. Air-fry at 330°F for 11 minutes or until toothpick inserted in center comes out clean.

8. Repeat step 7 to cook remaining 4 muffins.

Sheet Pan French Toast

Servings: 2

Cooking Time: 15 Minutes

Ingredients:

- Oil spray (hand-pumped)
- 2 large eggs
- ¼ cup milk
- 1 teaspoon vanilla extract
- ¼ teaspoon ground cinnamon
- 4 slices whole-grain bread
- ¾ cup maple syrup, or to taste

Directions:

1. Preheat the toaster oven on BAKE to 350°F for 5 minutes.
2. Line the baking tray with parchment paper and generously spray the paper with oil.
3. In a medium bowl, whisk the eggs, milk, vanilla, and cinnamon until well blended.
4. Dredge a slice of bread in the egg mixture until submerged, turn, and take it out. Gently shake the bread to remove any excess egg mixture and place the bread on the baking sheet. Repeat with the remaining bread.
5. Bake for 10 minutes.
6. Flip the bread and bake for 5 minutes longer until both sides are golden brown and crispy.
7. Serve with maple syrup.

Individual Overnight Omelets

Servings: 2

Cooking Time: 45 Minutes

Ingredients:

- 1 tablespoon unsalted butter, softened
- 2 slices hearty white sandwich bread
- 2 ounces cheddar cheese, shredded (½ cup)
- 3 large eggs
- ¾ cup whole milk
- 1 teaspoon minced fresh thyme or ¼ teaspoon dried
- ¼ teaspoon table salt
- ¼ teaspoon pepper

Directions:

1. Spray two 12-ounce ramekins with vegetable oil spray. Spread butter evenly over 1 side of bread slices, then cut into 1-inch pieces. Scatter half of bread evenly in prepared ramekins and sprinkle with half of cheddar. Repeat with remaining bread and cheese.

2. Whisk eggs, milk, thyme, salt, and pepper in bowl until well combined. Pour egg mixture evenly over bread and press lightly on bread to submerge. Wrap ramekins tightly with plastic wrap and refrigerate for at least 8 hours or up to 24 hours.

3. Adjust toaster oven rack to middle position and preheat the toaster oven to 350 degrees. Unwrap ramekins and place ramekins on small rimmed baking sheet. Bake until puffed and golden, 30 to 35 minutes, rotating sheet halfway through baking. Serve immediately.

Mushroom Blue Cheese Crostini

Servings: 10

Cooking Time: 3 Minutes

Ingredients:

- ➤ 1 tablespoon olive oil
- ➤ 8 ounces mushrooms, wild or button, sliced
- ➤ 3 cloves garlic, minced
- ➤ 2 tablespoons fresh flat-leaf (Italian) parsley, minced
- ➤ 2 teaspoons chopped fresh thyme, rosemary, or sage leaves
- ➤ Kosher salt and freshly ground black pepper
- ➤ 10 to 12 country bread, artisan bread, or baguette slices
- ➤ 1 cup grated fontina cheese
- ➤ ½ cup blue cheese or Gorgonzola crumbles
- ➤ 1 tablespoon fresh lemon juice
- ➤ Whole flat-leaf (Italian) parsley, for garnish

Directions:

1. Heat the olive oil in a medium nonstick skillet over medium-high heat. Add the mushrooms and cook, stirring frequently, until the liquid has evaporated, 7 to 10 minutes. Add the garlic and cook for 1 minute. Remove from the heat. Stir in the parsley and thyme and season with salt and pepper. Allow the mixture to cool.

2. Toast the slices of bread in the toaster oven.

3. Stir the fontina and blue cheese into the mushroom mixture.

4. Preheat the toaster oven on 400°F. Arrange the toasted baguette slices on a 12 x 12-inch baking sheet. Distribute the mushroom cheese mixture evenly over the toasted bread slices. Broil until the cheese melts, 2 to 3 minutes. Drizzle with the lemon juice. Garnish each crostini with a parsley leaf. Serve immediately.

Smoked Turkey, Walnut, And Pimiento Sandwich

Servings: 2

Cooking Time: 4 Minutes

Ingredients:

- Mixture:
- Stone-ground mustard
- 2 tablespoons canned diced pimientos
- 2 tablespoons finely chopped scallions
- 2 tablespoons finely chopped walnuts
- 2 tablespoons chopped raisins
- ½ teaspoon dill
- 2 tablespoons reduced-fat mayonnaise
- Salt and butcher's pepper to taste
- 4 slices rye bread
- 1 2.5-ounce package smoked turkey breast slices

Directions:

1. Combine the mixture ingredients and spread in equal portions on all bread slices. Layer 2 bread slices with equal portions of smoked turkey breast. Top with the other bread slices to make sandwiches.

2. TOAST twice on a broiling rack with a pan underneath.

Zucchini Walnut Bread

Servings: 6

Cooking Time: 30 Minutes

Ingredients:

- ¾ cup all-purpose flour
- ½ teaspoon baking soda
- 1 teaspoon ground cinnamon
- ⅛ teaspoon salt
- 1 large egg
- ⅓ cup packed brown sugar
- ¼ cup canola oil
- 1 teaspoon vanilla extract
- ⅓ cup milk
- 1 medium zucchini, shredded (about 1⅓ cups)
- ⅓ cup chopped walnuts

Directions:

1. Preheat the toaster oven to 320°F.
2. In a medium bowl, mix together the flour, baking soda, cinnamon, and salt.
3. In a large bowl, whisk together the egg, brown sugar, oil, vanilla, and milk. Stir in the zucchini.
4. Slowly fold the dry ingredients into the wet ingredients. Stir in the chopped walnuts. Then pour the batter into two 4-inch oven-safe loaf pans.
5. Bake for 30 minutes or until a toothpick inserted into the center comes out clean. Let cool before slicing.
6. Store tightly wrapped on the counter for up to 5 days, in the refrigerator for up to 10 days, or in the freezer for 3 months.

Spicy Beef Fajitas

Servings: 4

Cooking Time: 40 Minutes

Ingredients:

- Mixture:
- 1 pound flank steak, cut into thin strips
- 2 inches long
- 1 bell pepper, seeded and cut into thin strips
- 2 tablespoons chopped onion
- 1 tablespoon chopped fresh cilantro
- ¼ teaspoon hot sauce
- 1 teaspoon garlic powder
- ½ teaspoon cumin
- 1 teaspoon chili powder
- Salt and freshly ground black pepper to taste
- 4 8-inch flour tortillas

Directions:

1. Combine all the mixture ingredients in an oiled or nonstick 8½ × 8½ × 2-inch square baking (cake) pan.

2. BROIL for 20 minutes, turning every 5 minutes, or until the pepper and onion are tender and the meat is beginning to brown. Remove from the oven and place equal portions of the mixture in the center of each tortilla. Roll the tortilla around the mixture and lay, seam side down, in a shallow baking pan.

3. BAKE at 350° F. for 20 minutes, or until the tortillas are lightly browned.

Turkey And Tuna Melt

Servings: 2

Cooking Time: 4 Minutes

Ingredients:

- ➤ 4 slices multigrain bread Spicy brown mustard
- ➤ 1 6-ounce can tuna in water, drained well and crumbled
- ➤ ¼ pound thinly sliced turkey breast
- ➤ 4 slices low-fat Monterey Jack cheese
- ➤ 2 tablespoons finely chopped scallions
- ➤ Salt and freshly ground black pepper

Directions:

1. Spread one side of each bread slice with mustard and place on an oiled or nonstick
2. 6½ × 10-inch baking sheet.
3. Layer 2 slices with equal portions of tuna, turkey, cheese, and scallion. Season to taste with salt and pepper.
4. TOAST twice, or until the cheese is melted.

Hashbrown Potatoes Lyonnaise

Servings: 4

Cooking Time: 33 Minutes

Ingredients:

- 1 Vidalia (or other sweet) onion, sliced
- 1 teaspoon butter, melted
- 1 teaspoon brown sugar
- 2 large russet potatoes (about 1 pound), sliced ½-inch thick
- 1 tablespoon vegetable oil
- salt and freshly ground black pepper

Directions:

1. Preheat the toaster oven to 370°F.

2. Toss the sliced onions, melted butter and brown sugar together in the air fryer oven. Air-fry for 8 minutes, help the onions cook evenly.

3. While the onions are cooking, bring a 3-quart saucepan of salted water to a boil on the stovetop. Par-cook the potatoes in boiling water for 3 minutes. Drain the potatoes and pat them dry with a clean kitchen towel.

4. Add the potatoes to the onions in the air fryer oven and drizzle with vegetable oil. Toss to coat the potatoes with the oil and season with salt and freshly ground black pepper.

5. Increase the air fryer oven temperature to 400°F and air-fry for 22 minutes tossing the vegetables a few times during the cooking time to help the potatoes brown evenly. Season to taste again with salt and freshly ground black pepper and serve warm.

Cheddar Cheese Biscuits

Servings: 8   Cooking Time: 22 Minutes

Ingredients:

- 2⅓ cups self-rising flour
- 2 tablespoons sugar
- ½ cup butter (1 stick), frozen for 15 minutes
- ½ cup grated Cheddar cheese, plus more to melt on top
- 1⅓ cups buttermilk
- 1 cup all-purpose flour, for shaping
- 1 tablespoon butter, melted

Directions:

1. Line a buttered 7-inch metal cake pan with parchment paper or a silicone liner.

2. Combine the flour and sugar in a large mixing bowl. Grate the butter into the flour. Add the grated cheese and stir to coat the cheese and butter with flour. Then add the buttermilk and stir just until you can no longer see streaks of flour. The dough should be quite wet.

3. Spread the all-purpose (not self-rising) flour out on a small cookie sheet. With a spoon, scoop 8 evenly sized balls of dough into the flour, making sure they don't touch each other. With floured hands, coat each dough ball with flour and toss them gently from hand to hand to stir any excess flour. Place each floured dough ball into the prepared pan, right up next to the other. This will help the biscuits rise up, rather than spreading out.

4. Preheat the toaster oven to 380°F.

5. Transfer the cake pan to the air fryer oven, lowering it into the air fryer oven using a sling made of aluminum foil (fold a piece of aluminum foil into a strip about 2-inches wide by 24-inches long). Let the ends of the aluminum foil sling hang across the cake pan before returning to the air fryer oven.

6. Air-fry for 20 minutes. Check the biscuits a couple of times to make sure they are not getting too brown on top. If they are, re-arrange the aluminum foil strips to cover any brown parts. After 20 minutes, check the biscuits by inserting a toothpick into the center of the biscuits. It should come out clean. If it needs a little more time, continue to air-fry for a couple of extra minutes. Brush the tops of the biscuits with some melted butter and sprinkle a little more grated cheese on top if desired. Air-fry for another 2 minutes. Remove the cake pan from the air fryer oven using the aluminum sling. Let the biscuits cool for just a minute or two and then turn them out onto a plate and pull apart. Serve immediately.

FISH AND SEAFOOD

Lemon-roasted Salmon Fillets

Servings: 3

Cooking Time: 7 Minutes

Ingredients:

- ➢ 3 6-ounce skin-on salmon fillets
- ➢ Olive oil spray
- ➢ 9 Very thin lemon slices
- ➢ ¾ teaspoon Ground black pepper
- ➢ ¼ teaspoon Table salt

Directions:

1. Preheat the toaster oven to 400°F.

2. Generously coat the skin of each of the fillets with olive oil spray. Set the fillets skin side down on your work surface. Place three overlapping lemon slices down the length of each salmon fillet. Sprinkle them with the pepper and salt. Coat lightly with olive oil spray.

3. Use a nonstick-safe spatula to transfer the fillets one by one to the air fryer oven, leaving as much air space between them as possible. Air-fry undisturbed for 7 minutes, or until cooked through.

4. Use a nonstick-safe spatula to transfer the fillets to serving plates. Cool for only a minute or two before serving.

Almond-crusted Fish

Servings: 4

Cooking Time: 10 Minutes

Ingredients:

- 4 4-ounce fish fillets
- ¾ cup breadcrumbs
- ¼ cup sliced almonds, crushed
- 2 tablespoons lemon juice
- ⅛ teaspoon cayenne
- salt and pepper
- ¾ cup flour
- 1 egg, beaten with 1 tablespoon water
- oil for misting or cooking spray

Directions:

1. Split fish fillets lengthwise down the center to create 8 pieces.
2. Mix breadcrumbs and almonds together and set aside.
3. Mix the lemon juice and cayenne together. Brush on all sides of fish.
4. Season fish to taste with salt and pepper.
5. Place the flour on a sheet of wax paper.
6. Roll fillets in flour, dip in egg wash, and roll in the crumb mixture.
7. Mist both sides of fish with oil or cooking spray.
8. Spray air fryer oven and lay fillets inside.
9. Air-fry at 390°F for 5 minutes, turn fish over, and air-fry for an additional 5 minutes or until fish is done and flakes easily.

Crab-stuffed Peppers

Servings: 4

Cooking Time: 45 Minutes

Ingredients:

- ➢ Filling:
- ➢ 1½ cups fresh crabmeat, chopped, or 2 6-ounce cans lump crabmeat, drained
- ➢ 4 plum tomatoes, chopped
- ➢ 2 4-ounce cans sliced mushrooms, drained well
- ➢ 4 tablespoons pitted and sliced black olives
- ➢ 2 tablespoons olive oil
- ➢ 2 garlic cloves, minced
- ➢ ½ teaspoon ground cumin
- ➢ Salt and freshly ground black pepper to taste
- ➢ 4 large bell peppers, tops cut off, seeds and membrane removed
- ➢ ½ cup shredded low-fat mozzarella cheese

Directions:

1. Preheat the toaster oven to 375° F.

2. Combine the filling ingredients in a bowl and adjust the seasonings. Spoon the mixture to generously fill each pepper. Place the peppers upright in an 8½ × 8½ × 2-inch oiled or nonstick square (cake) pan.

3. BAKE for 40 minutes, or until the peppers are tender. Remove from the oven and sprinkle the cheese in equal portions on top of the peppers.

4. BROIL 5 minutes, or until the cheese is melted.

Marinated Catfish

Servings: 4

Cooking Time: 10 Minutes

Ingredients:

- ➤ Marinade:
- ➤ 1 tablespoon olive oil
- ➤ 1 tablespoon lemon juice
- ➤ ¼ dry white wine
- ➤ 1 tablespoon garlic powder
- ➤ 1 tablespoon soy sauce
- ➤ 4 6-ounce catfish fillets

Directions:

1. Combine the marinade ingredients in an 8½ × 8½ × 4-inch ovenproof baking dish. Add the fillets and let stand for 10 minutes, spooning the marinade over the fillets every 2 minutes.
2. BROIL the fillets for 15 minutes, or until the fish flakes easily with a fork.

Tex-mex Fish Tacos

Servings: 3

Cooking Time: 7 Minutes

Ingredients:

- ¾ teaspoon Chile powder
- ¼ teaspoon Ground cumin
- ¼ teaspoon Dried oregano
- 3 5-ounce skinless mahi-mahi fillets
- Vegetable oil spray
- 3 Corn or flour tortillas
- 6 tablespoons Diced tomatoes
- 3 tablespoons Regular, low-fat, or fat-free sour cream

Directions:

1. Preheat the toaster oven to 400°F.

2. Stir the chile powder, cumin, and oregano in a small bowl until well combined.

3. Coat each piece of fish all over (even the sides and ends) with vegetable oil spray. Sprinkle the spice mixture evenly over all sides of the fillets. Lightly spray them again.

4. When the machine is at temperature, set the fillets in the air fryer oven with as much air space between them as possible. Air-fry undisturbed for 7 minutes, until lightly browned and firm but not hard.

5. Use a nonstick-safe spatula to transfer the fillets to a wire rack. Microwave the tortillas on high for a few seconds, until supple. Put a fillet in each tortilla and top each with 2 tablespoons diced tomatoes and 1 tablespoon sour cream.

Tortilla-crusted Tilapia

Servings: 4

Cooking Time: 12 Minutes

Ingredients:

- 4 (5-ounce) tilapia fillets
- ½ teaspoon ground cumin
- Sea salt, for seasoning
- 1 cup tortilla chips, coarsely crushed
- Oil spray (hand-pumped)
- 1 lime, cut into wedges

Directions:

1. Preheat the toaster oven to 375°F on BAKE for 5 minutes.
2. Line the baking tray with parchment paper.
3. Lightly season the fish with the cumin and salt.
4. Press the tortilla chips onto the top of the fish fillets and place them on the baking sheet.
5. Lightly spray the fish with oil.
6. In position 2, bake until golden and just cooked through, about 12 minutes in total.
7. Serve with the lime wedges.

Best-dressed Trout

Servings: 2

Cooking Time: 25 Minutes

Ingredients:

- 2 dressed trout
- 1 egg, beaten
- 2 tablespoons finely ground almonds
- 2 tablespoons unbleached flour
- 1 teaspoon paprika or smoked paprika
- Pinch of salt (optional)
- 4 lemon slices, approximately ¼ inch thick
- 1 teaspoon lemon juice

Directions:

1. Preheat the toaster oven to 400° F.

2. Brush the trout (both sides) with the beaten egg. Blend the almonds, flour, paprika, and salt in a bowl and sprinkle both sides of the trout. Insert 2 lemon slices in each trout cavity and place the trout in an oiled or nonstick 8½ × 8½ × 2-inch square baking (cake) pan.

3. BAKE for 20 minutes, or until the meat is white and firm. Remove from the oven and turn the trout carefully with a spatula.

4. BROIL for 5 minutes, or until the trout is lightly browned.

Tuna Nuggets In Hoisin Sauce

Servings: 4

Cooking Time: 7 Minutes

Ingredients:

- ½ cup hoisin sauce
- 2 tablespoons rice wine vinegar
- 2 teaspoons sesame oil
- 1 teaspoon garlic powder
- 2 teaspoons dried lemongrass
- ¼ teaspoon red pepper flakes
- ½ small onion, quartered and thinly sliced
- 8 ounces fresh tuna, cut into 1-inch cubes
- cooking spray
- 3 cups cooked jasmine rice

Directions:

1. Mix the hoisin sauce, vinegar, sesame oil, and seasonings together.
2. Stir in the onions and tuna nuggets.
3. Spray air fryer oven baking pan with nonstick spray and pour in tuna mixture.
4. Air-fry at 390°F for 3 minutes. Stir gently.
5. Cook 2 minutes and stir again, checking for doneness. Tuna should be barely cooked through, just beginning to flake and still very moist. If necessary, continue cooking and stirring in 1-minute intervals until done.
6. Serve warm over hot jasmine rice.

Skewered Salsa Verde Shrimp

Servings: 4

Cooking Time: 8 Minutes

Ingredients:

- 1½ pounds large fresh shrimp, peeled and deveined
- Brushing mixture:
- 1 7-ounce can salsa verde
- 1 teaspoon ground cumin
- ½ teaspoon chopped fresh cilantro or parsley
- 1 teaspoon garlic powder
- 3 tablespoons plain yogurt
- 1 tablespoon olive oil
- Lemon wedges

Directions:

1. Thread the shrimp onto the skewers.

2. Combine the brushing mixture ingredients in a small bowl. Adjust the seasonings and brush the shrimp with the mixture.

3. BROIL the shrimp for 4 minutes. Turn the skewers, brush the shrimp again, and broil for another 4 minutes, or until the shrimp are firm and cooked. Remove the shrimp from the skewers and serve with lemon wedges.

Quick Shrimp Scampi

Servings: 2

Cooking Time: 5 Minutes

Ingredients:

- 16 to 20 raw large shrimp, peeled, deveined and tails removed
- ½ cup white wine
- freshly ground black pepper
- ¼ cup + 1 tablespoon butter, divided
- 1 clove garlic, sliced
- 1 teaspoon olive oil
- salt, to taste
- juice of ½ lemon, to taste
- ¼ cup chopped fresh parsley

Directions:

1. Start by marinating the shrimp in the white wine and freshly ground black pepper for at least 30 minutes, or as long as 2 hours in the refrigerator.

2. Preheat the toaster oven to 400°F.

3. Melt ¼ cup of butter in a small saucepan on the stovetop. Add the garlic and let the butter simmer, but be sure to not let it burn.

4. Pour the shrimp and marinade into the air fryer oven, letting the marinade drain through to the bottom drawer. Drizzle the olive oil on the shrimp and season well with salt. Air-fry at 400°F for 3 minutes. Turn the shrimp over and pour the garlic butter over the shrimp. Air-fry for another 2 minutes.

5. Remove the shrimp from the air fryer oven and transfer them to a bowl. Squeeze lemon juice over all the shrimp and toss with the chopped parsley and remaining tablespoon of butter. Season to taste with salt and serve immediately.

Crispy Pecan Fish

Servings: 4

Cooking Time: 20 Minutes

Ingredients:

- 3 tablespoons multigrain bread crumbs
- 3 tablespoons ground pecans
- 4 6-ounce fish fillets, approximately ¼ inch thick
- 1 egg white, whisked until frothy
- 1 tablespoon olive oil
- Salt and freshly ground black pepper to taste

Directions:

1. Combine the bread crumbs and pecans in a small bowl and transfer to a platter or plate.

2. Brush both sides of the fillets with egg white and dredge in the bread crumb/pecan mixture. Transfer the fillets to an oiled or nonstick 8½ × 8½ × 2-inch square baking (cake) pan.

3. BROIL for 10 minutes. Remove from the oven and carefully turn the fillets with a spatula. Broil again for 10 minutes, or until the fillets are lightly browned. Season to taste with the salt and pepper.

SNACKS APPETIZERS AND SIDES

Cheese Straws

Servings: 8

Cooking Time: 7 Minutes

Ingredients:

- For dusting All-purpose flour
- Two quarters of one thawed sheet (that is, a half of the sheet cut into two even pieces; wrap and refreeze the remainder) A 17.25-ounce box frozen puff pastry
- 1 Large egg(s)
- 2 tablespoons Water
- ¼ cup (about ¾ ounce) Finely grated Parmesan cheese
- up to 1 teaspoon Ground black pepper

Directions:

1. Preheat the toaster oven to 400°F.

2. Dust a clean, dry work surface with flour. Set one of the pieces of puff pastry on top, dust the pastry lightly with flour, and roll with a rolling pin to a 6-inch square.

3. Whisk the egg(s) and water in a small or medium bowl until uniform. Brush the pastry square(s) generously with this mixture. Sprinkle each square with 2 tablespoons grated cheese and up to ½ teaspoon ground black pepper.

4. Cut each square into 4 even strips. Grasp each end of 1 strip with clean, dry hands; twist it into a cheese straw. Place the twisted straws on a baking sheet.

5. Lay as many straws as will fit in the air-fryer oven—as a general rule, 4 of them in a small machine, 5 in a medium model, or 6 in a large. There should be space for air to circulate around the straws. Set the baking sheet with any remaining straws in the fridge.

6. Air-fry undisturbed for 7 minutes, or until puffed and crisp. Use tongs to transfer the cheese straws to a wire rack, then make subsequent batches in the same way (keeping the baking sheet with the remaining straws in the fridge as each batch cooks). Serve warm.

Roasted Brussels Sprouts Au Gratin

Servings: 6   Cooking Time: 36 Minutes

Ingredients:

- 1 pound fresh Brussels sprouts, trimmed and halved
- 2 tablespoons olive oil
- Kosher salt and freshly ground black pepper
- Nonstick cooking spray
- 2 slices bacon, cooked until crisp and crumbled
- 3 tablespoons unsalted butter
- 2 tablespoons all-purpose flour
- 1 cup whole milk
- 1 cup shredded Gruyère or Swiss cheese
- ½ teaspoon dried thyme leaves
- ¼ cup panko bread crumbs
- ¼ cup shredded Parmesan cheese

Directions:

1. Preheat the toaster oven to 450°F.

2. Toss the Brussels sprouts with the olive oil in a large bowl. Season with salt and pepper. Arrange the Brussels sprouts in a single layer in a 12 x 12-inch baking pan. Bake uncovered for 10 minutes. Stir and bake for an additional 8 to 10 minutes, or until the edges are beginning to char and the Brussels sprouts are just tender. Remove from the oven.

3. Reduce the toaster oven to 375°F. Spray a 1 ½-quart casserole dish or an 8 x 8-inch square baking pan with nonstick cooking spray. Place the Brussels sprouts in the casserole dish. Sprinkle with the crisp bacon.

4. Melt 2 tablespoons of the butter in a small saucepan over medium heat. Stir in the flour, blending until smooth and cook, stirring constantly, for 1 minute. Gradually add the milk and cook, stirring constantly, until the mixture is bubbly and thickened. Season with salt and pepper. Stir in the cheese and thyme and cook, stirring until melted. Pour the sauce over the Brussels sprouts.

5. Melt the remaining tablespoon of butter. Stir in the panko bread crumbs and Parmesan cheese. Sprinkle the bread crumb mixture over the casserole. Bake, uncovered, for 15 minutes or until golden brown and the edges are bubbling.

Turkey Bacon Dates

Servings: 16

Cooking Time: 7 Minutes

Ingredients:

- 16 whole, pitted dates
- 16 whole almonds
- 6 to 8 strips turkey bacon

Directions:

1. Stuff each date with a whole almond.
2. Depending on the size of your stuffed dates, cut bacon strips into halves or thirds. Each strip should be long enough to wrap completely around a date.
3. Wrap each date in a strip of bacon with ends overlapping and secure with toothpicks.
4. Place in air fryer oven and air-fry at 390°F for 7 minutes, until bacon is as crispy as you like.
5. Drain on paper towels or wire rack. Serve hot or at room temperature.

Sausage Cheese Pinwheels

Servings: 16

Cooking Time: 22 Minutes

Ingredients:

- 1 sheet frozen puff pastry, about 9 inches square, thawed (½ of a 17.3-ounce package)
- ½ pound bulk sausage
- ¾ cup shredded cheddar cheese

Directions:

1. Preheat the toaster oven to 400°F. Grease a 12 x 12-inch baking pan.

2. Unfold the puff pastry on a lightly floured surface and roll into a 10 x 12-inch rectangle. Carefully spread the sausage over the surface of the rectangle to within ½ inch of all four edges. Sprinkle the cheese evenly over the sausage. Starting with the long side, roll up tightly and press the edges to seal.

3. Using a serrated knife, slice the roll into ½-inch-thick pieces. You will get about 16 slices. Place the slices, cut side up, in the prepared baking pan. Bake for 18 to 22 minutes or until golden and the sausage is cooked through.

4. Serve warm or at room temperature.

Barbecue Chicken Nachos

Servings: 3

Cooking Time: 5 Minutes

Ingredients:

- 3 heaping cups (a little more than 3 ounces) Corn tortilla chips (gluten-free, if a concern)
- ¾ cup Shredded deboned and skinned rotisserie chicken meat (gluten-free, if a concern)
- 3 tablespoons Canned black beans, drained and rinsed
- 9 rings Pickled jalapeño slices
- 4 Small pickled cocktail onions, halved
- 3 tablespoons Barbecue sauce (any sort)
- ¾ cup (about 3 ounces) Shredded Cheddar cheese

Directions:

1. Preheat the toaster oven to 400°F.

2. Cut a circle of parchment paper to line a 6-inch round cake pan for a small air fryer oven, a 7-inch round cake pan for a medium air fryer oven, or an 8-inch round cake pan for a large machine.

3. Fill the pan with an even layer of about two-thirds of the chips. Sprinkle the chicken evenly over the chips. Set the pan in the air fryer oven and air-fry undisturbed for 2 minutes.

4. Remove the pan from the machine. Scatter the beans, jalapeño rings, and pickled onion halves over the chicken. Drizzle the barbecue sauce over everything, then sprinkle the cheese on top.

5. Return the pan to the machine and air-fry undisturbed for 3 minutes, or until the cheese has melted and is bubbly. Remove the pan from the machine and cool for a couple of minutes before serving.

Avocado Fries

Servings: 8

Cooking Time: 8 Minutes

Ingredients:

- 2 medium avocados, firm but ripe
- 1 large egg
- ½ teaspoon garlic powder
- ¼ teaspoon cayenne pepper
- ¼ teaspoon salt
- ¾ cup almond flour
- ½ cup finely grated Parmesan cheese
- ½ cup gluten-free breadcrumbs

Directions:

1. Preheat the toaster oven to 370°F.
2. Rinse the outside of the avocado with water. Slice the avocado in half, slice it in half again, and then slice it in half once more to get 8 slices. Remove the outer skin. Repeat for the other avocado. Set the avocado slices aside.
3. In a small bowl, whisk the egg, garlic powder, cayenne pepper, and salt in a small bowl. Set aside.
4. In a separate bowl, pour the almond flour.
5. In a third bowl, mix the Parmesan cheese and breadcrumbs.
6. Carefully roll the avocado slices in the almond flour, then dip them in the egg wash, and coat them in the cheese and breadcrumb topping. Repeat until all 16 fries are coated.
7. Liberally spray the air fryer oven with olive oil spray and place the avocado fries into the air fryer oven, leaving a little space around the sides between fries. Depending on the size of your air fryer oven, you may need to cook these in batches.
8. Cook fries for 8 minutes, or until the outer coating turns light brown.
9. Carefully remove, repeat with remaining slices, and then serve warm.

Buffalo Chicken Dip

Servings: 6

Cooking Time: 60 Minutes

Ingredients:

- 1 pound cream cheese
- ¾ cup Frank's RedHot Original Cayenne Pepper Sauce
- 3 cups shredded cooked chicken
- 1 cup ranch dressing
- 4 ounces blue cheese, crumbled (1 cup)
- 2 teaspoons Worcestershire sauce
- 4 ounces sharp cheddar cheese, shredded (1 cup)
- 2 scallions, sliced thin

Directions:

1. Adjust toaster oven rack to middle position and preheat the toaster oven to 350 degrees. Combine cream cheese and hot sauce in medium bowl and microwave until cream cheese is very soft, about 2 minutes, whisking halfway through microwaving. Whisk until smooth and no lumps of cream cheese remain. Stir in chicken, dressing, blue cheese, and Worcestershire until combined (visible bits of blue cheese are OK).

2. Transfer mixture to 2-quart baking dish and smooth top with rubber spatula. Bake for 20 minutes. Remove dish from toaster oven, stir dip, and sprinkle with cheddar. Return dish to oven and continue to bake until cheddar is melted and dip is bubbling around edges, 15 to 20 minutes longer. Transfer dish to wire rack and let cool for 10 minutes. Sprinkle with scallions and serve.

Cajun Roasted Okra

Servings: 4-6

Cooking Time: 40 Minutes

Ingredients:

- ➢ 1 pound okra, tops removed and sliced in half lengthwise
- ➢ 2 Tablespoons olive oil
- ➢ 1 teaspoon Cajun seasoning
- ➢ 1/2 teaspoon black pepper
- ➢ Sea salt to taste
- ➢ Cajun Dipping Sauce

Directions:

1. Preheat the toaster oven to 450°F.
2. Line a 15X9X1-inch baking pan with aluminum foil and spray with nonstick cooking spray.
3. Place okra, olive oil, Cajun seasoning, pepper and salt in prepared pan; stir until well coated.
4. Bake 35 to 40 minutes or until okra is crisp.
5. Serve with Cajun Dipping Sauce.

Polenta Fries With Chili-lime Mayo

Servings: 4

Cooking Time: 28 Minutes

Ingredients:

- 2 teaspoons vegetable or olive oil
- ¼ teaspoon paprika
- 1 pound prepared polenta, cut into 3-inch x ½-inch sticks
- salt and freshly ground black pepper
- Chili-Lime Mayo
- ½ cup mayonnaise
- 1 teaspoon chili powder
- ¼ teaspoon ground cumin
- juice of half a lime
- 1 teaspoon chopped fresh cilantro
- salt and freshly ground black pepper

Directions:

1. Preheat the toaster oven to 400°F.

2. Combine the oil and paprika and then carefully toss the polenta sticks in the mixture.

3. Air-fry the polenta fries at 400°F for 15 minutes. Rotate the fries and continue to air-fry for another 13 minutes or until the fries have browned nicely. Season to taste with salt and freshly ground black pepper.

4. To make the chili-lime mayo, combine all the ingredients in a small bowl and stir well.

5. Serve the polenta fries warm with chili-lime mayo on the side for dipping.

Eggs In Avocado Halves

Servings: 3

Cooking Time: 23 Minutes

Ingredients:

- ➢ 3 Hass avocados, halved and pitted but not peeled
- ➢ 6 Medium eggs
- ➢ Vegetable oil spray
- ➢ 3 tablespoons Heavy or light cream (not fat-free cream)
- ➢ To taste Table salt
- ➢ To taste Ground black pepper

Directions:

1. Preheat the toaster oven to 350°F .

2. Slice a small amount off the (skin) side of each avocado half so it can sit stable, without rocking. Lightly coat the skin of the avocado half (the side that will now sit stable) with vegetable oil spray.

3. Arrange the avocado halves open side up on a cutting board, then crack an egg into the indentation in each where the pit had been. If any white overflows the avocado half, wipe that bit of white off the cut edge of the avocado before proceeding.

4. Remove the pan (or its attachment) from the machine and set the filled avocado halves in it in one layer. Return it to the machine without pushing it in. Drizzle each avocado half with about 1½ teaspoons cream, a little salt, and a little ground black pepper.

5. Air-fry undisturbed for 10 minutes for a soft-set yolk, or air-fry for 13 minutes for more-set eggs.

6. Use a nonstick-safe spatula and a flatware fork for balance to transfer the avocado halves to serving plates. Cool a minute or two before serving.

Skinny Fries

Servings: 2

Cooking Time: 15 Minutes

Ingredients:

- 2 to 3 russet potatoes, peeled and cut into ¼-inch sticks
- 2 to 3 teaspoons olive or vegetable oil
- salt

Directions:

1. Cut the potatoes into ¼-inch strips. (A mandolin with a julienne blade is really helpful here.) Rinse the potatoes with cold water several times and let them soak in cold water for at least 10 minutes or as long as overnight.

2. Preheat the toaster oven to 380°F.

3. Drain and dry the potato sticks really well, using a clean kitchen towel. Toss the fries with the oil in a bowl and then air-fry the fries in two batches at 380°F for 15 minutes.

4. Add the first batch of French fries back into the air fryer oven with the finishing batch and let everything warm through for a few minutes. As soon as the fries are done, season them with salt and transfer to a plate. Serve them warm with ketchup or your favorite dip.

Crab Rangoon Dip With Wonton Chips

Servings: 6   Cooking Time: 18 Minutes

Ingredients:

- Wonton Chips:
- 1 (12-ounce) package wonton wrappers
- vegetable oil
- sea salt
- Crab Rangoon Dip:
- 8 ounces cream cheese, softened
- ¾ cup sour cream
- 1 teaspoon Worcestershire sauce
- 1½ teaspoons soy sauce
- 1 teaspoon sesame oil
- ⅛ teaspoon ground cayenne pepper
- ¼ teaspoon salt
- freshly ground black pepper
- 8 ounces cooked crabmeat
- 1 cup grated white Cheddar cheese
- ⅓ cup chopped scallions
- paprika (for garnish)

Directions:

1. Cut the wonton wrappers in half diagonally to form triangles. Working in batches, lay the wonton triangles on a flat surface and brush or spray both sides with vegetable oil.

2. Preheat the toaster oven to 370°F.

3. Place about 10 to 12 wonton triangles in the air fryer oven, letting them overlap slightly. Air-fry for just 2 minutes. Transfer the wonton chips to a large bowl and season immediately with sea salt. (You'll hear the chips start to spin around in the air fryer oven when they are almost done.) Repeat with the rest of wontons (keeping those fishing hands at bay!).

4. To make the dip, combine the cream cheese, sour cream, Worcestershire sauce, soy sauce, sesame oil, cayenne pepper, salt, and freshly ground black pepper in a bowl. Mix well and then fold in the crabmeat, Cheddar cheese, and scallions.

5. Transfer the dip to a 7-inch ceramic baking pan or shallow casserole dish. Sprinkle paprika on top and cover the dish with aluminum foil. Lower the dish into the air fryer oven using a sling made of aluminum foil (fold a piece of aluminum foil into a strip about 2-inches wide by 24-inches long). Air-fry for 11 minutes. Remove the aluminum foil and air-fry for another 5 minutes to finish cooking and brown the top. Serve hot with the wonton chips.

POULTRY

Mediterranean Stuffed Chicken Breasts

Servings: 4

Cooking Time: 24 Minutes

Ingredients:

- ➤ 4 boneless, skinless chicken breasts
- ➤ ½ teaspoon salt
- ➤ ½ teaspoon black pepper
- ➤ ½ teaspoon garlic powder
- ➤ ½ teaspoon paprika
- ➤ ½ cup canned artichoke hearts, chopped
- ➤ 4 ounces cream cheese
- ➤ ¼ cup grated Parmesan cheese

Directions:

1. Pat the chicken breasts with a paper towel. Using a sharp knife, cut a pouch in the side of each chicken breast for filling.

2. In a small bowl, mix the salt, pepper, garlic powder, and paprika. Season the chicken breasts with this mixture.

3. In a medium bowl, mix together the artichokes, cream cheese, and grated Parmesan cheese. Divide the filling between the 4 breasts, stuffing it inside the pouches. Use toothpicks to close the pouches and secure the filling.

4. Preheat the toaster oven to 360°F.

5. Spray the air fryer oven liberally with cooking spray, add the stuffed chicken breasts to the air fryer oven, and spray liberally with cooking spray again. Air-fry for 14 minutes, carefully turn over the chicken breasts, and cook another 10 minutes. Check the temperature at 20 minutes cooking. Chicken breasts are fully cooked when the center measures 165°F. Cook in batches, if needed.

Chicken Souvlaki Gyros

Servings: 4

Cooking Time: 18 Minutes

Ingredients:

- ¼ cup extra-virgin olive oil
- 1 clove garlic, crushed
- 1 tablespoon Italian seasoning
- ½ teaspoon paprika
- ½ lemon, sliced
- ¼ teaspoon salt
- 1 pound boneless, skinless chicken breasts
- 4 whole-grain pita breads
- 1 cup shredded lettuce
- ½ cup chopped tomatoes
- ¼ cup chopped red onion
- ¼ cup cucumber yogurt sauce

Directions:

1. In a large resealable plastic bag, combine the olive oil, garlic, Italian seasoning, paprika, lemon, and salt. Add the chicken to the bag and secure shut. Vigorously shake until all the ingredients are combined. Set in the fridge for 2 hours to marinate.

2. When ready to cook, preheat the toaster oven to 360°F.

3. Liberally spray the air fryer oven with olive oil mist. Remove the chicken from the bag and discard the leftover marinade. Place the chicken into the air fryer oven, allowing enough room between the chicken breasts to flip.

4. Air-fry for 10 minutes, flip, and cook another 8 minutes.

5. Remove the chicken from the air fryer oven when it has cooked (or the internal temperature of the chicken reaches 165°F). Let rest 5 minutes. Then thinly slice the chicken into strips.

6. Assemble the gyros by placing the pita bread on a flat surface and topping with chicken, lettuce, tomatoes, onion, and a drizzle of yogurt sauce.

7. Serve warm.

Gluten-free Nutty Chicken Fingers

Servings: 4

Cooking Time: 10 Minutes

Ingredients:

- ½ cup gluten-free flour
- ½ teaspoon garlic powder
- ¼ teaspoon onion powder
- ¼ teaspoon black pepper
- ¼ teaspoon salt
- 1 cup walnuts, pulsed into coarse flour
- ½ cup gluten-free breadcrumbs
- 2 large eggs
- 1 pound boneless, skinless chicken tenders

Directions:

1. Preheat the toaster oven to 400°F.
2. In a medium bowl, mix the flour, garlic, onion, pepper, and salt. Set aside.
3. In a separate bowl, mix the walnut flour and breadcrumbs.
4. In a third bowl, whisk the eggs.
5. Liberally spray the air fryer oven with olive oil spray.
6. Pat the chicken tenders dry with a paper towel. Dredge the tenders one at a time in the flour, then dip them in the egg, and toss them in the breadcrumb coating. Repeat until all tenders are coated.
7. Set each tender in the air fryer oven, leaving room on each side of the tender to allow for flipping.
8. When the air fryer oven is full, cook 5 minutes, flip, and cook another 5 minutes. Check the internal temperature after cooking completes; it should read 165°F. If it does not, cook another 2 to 4 minutes.
9. Remove the tenders and let cool 5 minutes before serving. Repeat until all the tenders are cooked.

Apricot Glazed Chicken Thighs

Servings: 2

Cooking Time: 22 Minutes

Ingredients:

- 4 bone-in chicken thighs (about 2 pounds)
- olive oil
- 1 teaspoon salt
- ¼ teaspoon freshly ground black pepper
- ½ teaspoon onion powder
- ¾ cup apricot preserves 1½ tablespoons Dijon mustard
- ½ teaspoon dried thyme
- 1 teaspoon soy sauce
- fresh thyme leaves, for garnish

Directions:

1. Preheat the toaster oven to 380°F.

2. Brush or spray both the air fryer oven and the chicken with the olive oil. Combine the salt, pepper and onion powder and season both sides of the chicken with the spice mixture.

3. Place the seasoned chicken thighs, skin side down in the air fryer oven. Air-fry for 10 minutes.

4. While chicken is cooking, make the glaze by combining the apricot preserves, Dijon mustard, thyme and soy sauce in a small bowl.

5. When the time is up on the air fryer oven, spoon half of the apricot glaze over the chicken thighs and air-fry for 2 minutes. Then flip the chicken thighs over so that the skin side is facing up and air-fry for an additional 8 minutes. Finally, spoon and spread the rest of the glaze evenly over the chicken thighs and air-fry for a final 2 minutes. Transfer the chicken to a serving platter and sprinkle the fresh thyme leaves on top.

Orange-glazed Roast Chicken

Servings: 6

Cooking Time: 100 Minutes

Ingredients:

- 1 3-pound whole chicken, rinsed and patted dry with paper towels
- Brushing mixture:
- 2 tablespoons orange juice concentrate
- 1 tablespoon soy sauce
- 1 tablespoon toasted sesame oil
- 1 teaspoon ground ginger
- Salt and freshly ground black pepper to taste

Directions:

1. Preheat the toaster oven to 400° F.

2. Place the chicken, breast side up, in an oiled or nonstick 8½ × 8½ × 2-inch square (cake) pan and brush with the mixture, which has been combined in a small bowl, reserving the remaining mixture. Cover with aluminum foil.

3. BAKE for 1 hour and 20 minutes. Uncover and brush the chicken with remaining mixture.

4. BAKE, uncovered, for 20 minutes, or until the breast is tender when pierced with a fork and golden brown.

Crispy Curry Chicken Tenders

Servings: 4

Cooking Time: 14 Minutes

Ingredients:

- 1 pound boneless skinless chicken tenders
- ¼ cup plain yogurt
- 2 tablespoons thai red curry paste
- 1½ teaspoons salt, divided
- ½ teaspoon pepper
- 1¾ cups panko breadcrumbs
- 1 teaspoon granulated garlic
- 1 teaspoon granulated onion
- Olive oil or avocado oil spray

Directions:

1. Whisk together the yogurt, curry paste, 1 teaspoon of salt, and pepper in a large bowl. Add the chicken tenders and toss to coat. Cover bowl with plastic wrap and marinate in the fridge for 6-8 hours.

2. Combine the panko breadcrumbs, ½ teaspoon salt, garlic, and onion. Remove chicken tenders from the marinade and coat individually in the panko mixture.

3. Preheat the toaster oven to 430°F.

4. Spray both sides of each chicken tender well with olive oil or avocado oil spray, then place into the fry basket.

5. Insert the fry basket at mid position in the preheated oven.

6. Select the Air Fry and Shake functions, adjust time to 14 minutes, and press Start/Pause.

7. Flip chicken tenders halfway through cooking. The Shake Reminder will let you know when.

8. Remove when chicken tenders are golden and crispy.

Coconut Chicken With Apricot-ginger Sauce

Servings: 4   Cooking Time: 8 Minutes

Ingredients:

- 1½ pounds boneless, skinless chicken tenders, cut in large chunks (about 1¼ inches)
- salt and pepper
- ½ cup cornstarch
- 2 eggs
- 1 tablespoon milk
- 3 cups shredded coconut (see below)
- oil for misting or cooking spray
- Apricot-Ginger Sauce
- ½ cup apricot preserves
- 2 tablespoons white vinegar
- ¼ teaspoon ground ginger
- ¼ teaspoon low-sodium soy sauce
- 2 teaspoons white or yellow onion, grated or finely minced

Directions:

1. Mix all ingredients for the Apricot-Ginger Sauce well and let sit for flavors to blend while you cook the chicken.

2. Season chicken chunks with salt and pepper to taste.

3. Place cornstarch in a shallow dish.

4. In another shallow dish, beat together eggs and milk.

5. Place coconut in a third shallow dish. (If also using panko breadcrumbs, as suggested below, stir them to mix well.)

6. Spray air fryer oven with oil or cooking spray.

7. Dip each chicken chunk into cornstarch, shake off excess, and dip in egg mixture.

8. Shake off excess egg mixture and roll lightly in coconut or coconut mixture. Spray with oil.

9. Place coated chicken chunks in air fryer oven in a single layer, close together but without sides touching.

10. Air-fry at 360°F for 4 minutes, stop, and turn chunks over.

11. Cook an additional 4 minutes or until chicken is done inside and coating is crispy brown.

12. Repeat steps 9 through 11 to cook remaining chicken chunks.

Fiesta Chicken Plate

Servings: 4

Cooking Time: 15 Minutes

Ingredients:

- 1 pound boneless, skinless chicken breasts (2 large breasts)
- 2 tablespoons lime juice
- 1 teaspoon cumin
- ½ teaspoon salt
- ½ cup grated Pepper Jack cheese
- 1 16-ounce can refried beans
- ½ cup salsa
- 2 cups shredded lettuce
- 1 medium tomato, chopped
- 2 avocados, peeled and sliced
- 1 small onion, sliced into thin rings
- sour cream
- tortilla chips (optional)

Directions:

1. Split each chicken breast in half lengthwise.
2. Mix lime juice, cumin, and salt together and brush on all surfaces of chicken breasts.
3. Place in air fryer oven and air-fry at 390°F for 15 minutes, until well done.
4. Divide the cheese evenly over chicken breasts and air-fry for an additional minute to melt cheese.
5. While chicken is cooking, heat refried beans on stovetop or in microwave.
6. When ready to serve, divide beans among 4 plates. Place chicken breasts on top of beans and spoon salsa over. Arrange the lettuce, tomatoes, and avocados artfully on each plate and scatter with the onion rings.
7. Pass sour cream at the table and serve with tortilla chips if desired.

Teriyaki Chicken Drumsticks

Servings: 2

Cooking Time: 17 Minutes

Ingredients:

- 2 tablespoons soy sauce
- ¼ cup dry sherry
- 1 tablespoon brown sugar
- 2 tablespoons water
- 1 tablespoon rice wine vinegar
- 1 clove garlic, crushed
- 1-inch fresh ginger, peeled and sliced
- pinch crushed red pepper flakes
- 4 to 6 bone-in, skin-on chicken drumsticks
- 1 tablespoon cornstarch
- fresh cilantro leaves

Directions:

1. Make the marinade by combining the soy sauce, dry sherry, brown sugar, water, rice vinegar, garlic, ginger and crushed red pepper flakes. Pour the marinade over the chicken legs, cover and let the chicken marinate for 1 to 4 hours in the refrigerator.

2. Preheat the toaster oven to 380°F.

3. Transfer the chicken from the marinade to the air fryer oven, transferring any extra marinade to a small saucepan. Air-fry at 380°F for 8 minutes. Flip the chicken over and continue to air-fry for another 6 minutes, watching to make sure it doesn't brown too much.

4. While the chicken is cooking, bring the reserved marinade to a simmer on the stovetop. Dissolve the cornstarch in 2 tablespoons of water and stir this into the saucepan. Bring to a boil to thicken the sauce. Remove the garlic clove and slices of ginger from the sauce and set aside.

5. When the time is up on the air fryer oven, brush the thickened sauce on the chicken and air-fry for 3 more minutes. Remove the chicken from the air fryer oven and brush with the remaining sauce.

6. Serve over rice and sprinkle the cilantro leaves on top.

Chicken Pot Pie

Servings: 4

Cooking Time: 65 Minutes

Ingredients:

- ¼ cup salted butter
- 1 small sweet onion, chopped
- 1 carrot, chopped
- 1 teaspoon minced garlic
- ¼ cup all-purpose flour
- 1 cup low-sodium chicken broth
- ¼ cup heavy (whipping) cream
- 2 cups diced store-bought rotisserie chicken
- 1 cup frozen peas
- Sea salt, for seasoning
- Freshly ground black pepper, for seasoning
- 1 unbaked store-bought pie crust

Directions:

1. Place the rack in position 1 and preheat the toaster oven to 350°F on BAKE for 5 minutes.

2. Melt the butter in a large saucepan over medium-high heat. Sauté the onion, carrot, and garlic until softened, about 12 minutes. Whisk in the flour to form a thick paste and whisk for 1 minute to cook.

3. Add the broth and whisk until thickened, about 2 minutes. Add the heavy cream, whisking to combine. Add the chicken and peas, and season with salt and pepper.

4. Transfer the filling to a 1½-quart casserole dish and top with the pie crust, tucking the edges into the sides of the casserole dish to completely enclose the filling. Cut 4 or 5 slits in the top of the crust.

5. Bake for 50 minutes until the crust is golden brown and the filling is bubbly. Serve.

Sticky Soy Chicken Thighs

Servings: 2

Cooking Time: 20 Minutes

Ingredients:

- 2 tablespoons less-sodium soy sauce
- 1 tablespoon olive oil
- 1 tablespoon honey
- 1 tablespoon balsamic vinegar
- 1 tablespoon chili sauce
- Juice of 1 lime
- 1 teaspoon minced garlic
- 1 teaspoon ginger, peeled and grated
- 2 bone-in, skin-on chicken thighs
- Oil spray (hand-pumped)
- 1 scallion, both white and green parts, thinly sliced, for garnish
- 2 teaspoons sesame seeds, for garnish

Directions:

1. Preheat the toaster oven to 400°F on AIR FRY for 5 minutes.

2. In a large bowl, combine the soy sauce, olive oil, honey, balsamic vinegar, chili sauce, lime juice, garlic, and ginger. Add the chicken thighs to the bowl and toss to coat. Cover the bowl and refrigerate for 30 minutes.

3. Place the air-fryer basket in the baking tray and generously spray with oil.

4. Place the thighs in the basket, and in position 2, air fry for 20 minutes until cooked through and the thighs are browned and lightly caramelized, with an internal temperature of 165°F.

5. Garnish the chicken with the scallion and sesame seeds and serve.

Crispy Chicken Tenders

Servings: 4

Cooking Time: 22 Minutes

Ingredients:

- 1 pound boneless, skinless chicken breasts
- ½ cup all-purpose flour
- ½ teaspoon kosher salt
- ¼ teaspoon freshly ground black ground pepper
- 1 large egg, beaten
- 3 tablespoons whole milk
- 1 cup cornflake crumbs
- ½ cup grated Parmesan cheese
- Nonstick cooking spray

Directions:

1. Preheat the toaster oven to 375°F. Line a 12 x 12-inch baking pan with nonstick aluminum foil. (Or if lining the pan with regular foil, spray it with nonstick cooking spray.)

2. Cover the chicken with plastic wrap. Pound the chicken with the flat side of a meat pounder until it is even and about ½ inch thick. Cut the chicken into strips about 1 by 3 inches.

3. Combine the flour, salt, and pepper in a small shallow dish. Place the egg and milk in another small shallow dish and use a fork to combine. Place the cornflake crumbs and Parmesan in a third small shallow dish and combine.

4. Dredge each chicken piece in the flour, then dip in the egg mixture, and then coat with the cornflake crumb mixture. Place the chicken strips in a single layer in the prepared baking pan. Spray the chicken strips generously with nonstick cooking spray.

5. Bake for 10 minutes. Turn the chicken and spray with nonstick cooking spray. Bake for an additional 10 to 12 minutes, or until crisp and a meat thermometer registers 165 ºF.

BEEF PORK AND LAMB

Cilantro-crusted Flank Steak

Servings: 2

Cooking Time: 16 Minutes

Ingredients:

- Coating:
- 2 tablespoons chopped onion
- 1 tablespoon olive oil
- 2 tablespoons plain nonfat yogurt
- 1 plum tomato
- ½ cup fresh cilantro leaves
- 2 tablespoons cooking sherry
- ¼ teaspoon hot sauce
- 1 teaspoon garlic powder
- ½ teaspoon chili powder
- Salt and freshly ground black pepper
- 2 8-ounce flank steaks

Directions:

1. Process the coating ingredients in a blender or food processor until smooth. Spread half of the coating mixture on top of the flank steaks. Place the steaks on a broiling rack with a pan underneath.

2. BROIL for 8 minutes. Turn with tongs, spread the remaining mixture on the steaks, and broil again for 8 minutes, or until done to your preference.

Pretzel-coated Pork Tenderloin

Servings: 4

Cooking Time: 10 Minutes

Ingredients:

- 1 Large egg white(s)
- 2 teaspoons Dijon mustard (gluten-free, if a concern)
- 1½ cups (about 6 ounces) Crushed pretzel crumbs
- 1 pound (4 sections) Pork tenderloin, cut into ¼-pound (4-ounce) sections
- Vegetable oil spray

Directions:

1. Preheat the toaster oven to 350°F .

2. Set up and fill two shallow soup plates or small pie plates on your counter: one for the egg white(s), whisked with the mustard until foamy; and one for the pretzel crumbs.

3. Dip a section of pork tenderloin in the egg white mixture and turn it to coat well, even on the ends. Let any excess egg white mixture slip back into the rest, then set the pork in the pretzel crumbs. Roll it several times, pressing gently, until the pork is evenly coated, even on the ends. Generously coat the pork section with vegetable oil spray, set it aside, and continue coating and spraying the remaining sections.

4. Set the pork sections in the air fryer oven with at least ¼ inch between them. Air-fry undisturbed for 10 minutes, or until an instant-read meat thermometer inserted into the center of one section registers 145°F.

5. Use kitchen tongs to transfer the pieces to a wire rack. Cool for 3 to 5 minutes before serving.

Bourbon Broiled Steak

Servings: 2

Cooking Time: 14 Minutes

Ingredients:

- Brushing mixture:
- ¼ cup bourbon
- 1 teaspoon garlic powder
- 1 tablespoon olive oil
- 1 teaspoon soy sauce
- 2 6- to 8-ounce sirloin steaks, ¾ inch thick

Directions:

1. Combine the brushing mixture ingredients in a small bowl. Brush the steaks on both sides with the mixture and place on the broiling rack with a pan underneath.

2. BROIL 4 minutes, remove from the oven, turn with tongs, brush the top and sides, and broil again for 4 minutes, or until done to your preference. To use the brushing mixture as a sauce or gravy, pour the mixture into a baking pan.

3. BROIL the mixture for 6 minutes, or until it begins to bubble.

Crispy Smoked Pork Chops

Servings: 3

Cooking Time: 8 Minutes

Ingredients:

➢ ⅔ cup All-purpose flour or tapioca flour

➢ 1 Large egg white(s)

➢ 2 tablespoons Water

➢ 1½ cups Corn flake crumbs (gluten-free, if a concern)

➢ 3 ½-pound, ½-inch-thick bone-in smoked pork chops

Directions:

1. Preheat the toaster oven to 375°F.

2. Set up and fill three shallow soup plates or small pie plates on your counter: one for the flour; one for the egg white(s), whisked with the water until foamy; and one for the corn flake crumbs.

3. Set a chop in the flour and turn it several times, coating both sides and the edges. Gently shake off any excess flour, then set it in the beaten egg white mixture. Turn to coat both sides as well as the edges. Let any excess egg white slip back into the rest, then set the chop in the corn flake crumbs. Turn it several times, pressing gently to coat the chop evenly on both sides and around the edge. Set the chop aside and continue coating the remaining chop(s) in the same way.

4. Set the chops in the air fryer oven with as much air space between them as possible. Air-fry undisturbed for 8 minutes, or until the coating is crunchy and the chops are heated through.

5. Use kitchen tongs to transfer the chops to a wire rack and cool for a couple of minutes before serving.

Steak With Herbed Butter

Servings: 2

Cooking Time: 16 Minutes

Ingredients:

- 4 tablespoons unsalted butter, softened
- 1 tablespoon minced flat-leaf (Italian) parsley
- 1 tablespoon chopped fresh chives
- 2 cloves garlic, minced
- 1 teaspoon Worcestershire sauce
- 2 beef strip steaks, cut about 1 ½ inches thick
- 1 tablespoon olive oil
- Kosher salt and freshly ground black pepper

Directions:

1. Combine the butter, parsley, chives, garlic, and Worcestershire sauce in a small bowl until well blended; set aside.

2. Preheat the toaster oven to broil.

3. Brush the steaks with olive oil and season with salt and pepper. Place the steak on the broiler rack set over the broiler pan. Place the pan in the toaster oven, positioning the steaks about 3 to 4 inches below the heating element. (Depending on your oven and the thickness of the steak, you may need to set the rack to the middle position.) Broil for 6 minutes, turn the steaks over, and broil for an additional 7 minutes. If necessary to reach the desired doneness, turn the steaks over again and broil for an additional 3 minutes or until you reach your desired doneness.

4. Spread the herb butter generously over the steaks. Allow the steaks to stand for 5 to 10 minutes before slicing and serving.

Ribeye Steak With Blue Cheese Compound Butter

Servings: 2

Cooking Time: 12 Minutes

Ingredients:

- 5 tablespoons unsalted butter, softened
- ¼ cup crumbled blue cheese 2 teaspoons lemon juice
- 1 tablespoon freshly chopped chives
- Salt & freshly ground black pepper, to taste
- 2 (12 ounce) boneless ribeye steaks

Directions:

1. Mix together butter, blue cheese, lemon juice, and chives until smooth.
2. Season the butter to taste with salt and pepper.
3. Place the butter on plastic wrap and form into a 3-inch log, tying the ends of the plastic wrap together.
4. Place the butter in the fridge for 4 hours to harden.
5. Allow the steaks to sit at room temperature for 1 hour.
6. Pat the steaks dry with paper towels and season to taste with salt and pepper.
7. Insert the fry basket at top position in the Cosori Smart Air Fryer Toaster Oven.
8. Preheat the toaster Oven to 450°F.
9. Place the steaks in the fry basket in the preheated oven.
10. Select the Broil function, adjust time to 12 minutes, and press Start/Pause.
11. Remove when done and allow to rest for 5 minutes.
12. Remove the butter from the fridge, unwrap, and slice into ¾-inch pieces.
13. Serve the steak with one or two pieces of sliced compound butter.

Pork Loin

Servings: 8

Cooking Time: 50 Minutes

Ingredients:

- 1 tablespoon lime juice
- 1 tablespoon orange marmalade
- 1 teaspoon coarse brown mustard
- 1 teaspoon curry powder
- 1 teaspoon dried lemongrass
- 2-pound boneless pork loin roast
- salt and pepper
- cooking spray

Directions:

1. Mix together the lime juice, marmalade, mustard, curry powder, and lemongrass.
2. Rub mixture all over the surface of the pork loin. Season to taste with salt and pepper.
3. Spray air fryer oven with nonstick spray and place pork roast diagonally in the pan.
4. Air-fry at 360°F for approximately 50 minutes, until roast registers 130°F on a meat thermometer.
5. Wrap roast in foil and let rest for 10minutes before slicing.

Red Curry Flank Steak

Servings: 4

Cooking Time: 18 Minutes

Ingredients:

- 3 tablespoons red curry paste
- ¼ cup olive oil
- 2 teaspoons grated fresh ginger
- 2 tablespoons soy sauce
- 2 tablespoons rice wine vinegar
- 3 scallions, minced
- 1½ pounds flank steak
- fresh cilantro (or parsley) leaves

Directions:

1. Mix the red curry paste, olive oil, ginger, soy sauce, rice vinegar and scallions together in a bowl. Place the flank steak in a shallow glass dish and pour half the marinade over the steak. Pierce the steak several times with a fork or meat tenderizer to let the marinade penetrate the meat. Turn the steak over, pour the remaining marinade over the top and pierce the steak several times again. Cover and marinate the steak in the refrigerator for 6 to 8 hours.

2. When you are ready to cook, remove the steak from the refrigerator and let it sit at room temperature for 30 minutes.

3. Preheat the toaster oven to 400°F.

4. Cut the flank steak in half so that it fits more easily into the air fryer oven and transfer both pieces to the air fryer oven. Pour the marinade over the steak. Air-fry for 18 minutes, depending on your preferred degree of doneness of the steak (12 minutes = medium rare). Flip the steak over halfway through the cooking time.

5. When your desired degree of doneness has been reached, remove the steak to a cutting board and let it rest for 5 minutes before slicing. Thinly slice the flank steak against the grain of the meat. Transfer the slices to a serving platter, pour any juice from the bottom of the air fryer oven over the sliced flank steak and sprinkle the fresh cilantro on top.

Lamb Burger With Feta And Olives

Servings: 3   Cooking Time: 16 Minutes

Ingredients:

- 2 teaspoons olive oil
- ⅓ onion, finely chopped
- 1 clove garlic, minced
- 1 pound ground lamb
- 2 tablespoons fresh parsley, finely chopped
- 1½ teaspoons fresh oregano, finely chopped
- ½ cup black olives, finely chopped
- ⅓ cup crumbled feta cheese
- ½ teaspoon salt
- freshly ground black pepper
- 4 thick pita breads
- toppings and condiments

Directions:

1. Preheat a medium skillet over medium-high heat on the stovetop. Add the olive oil and cook the onion until tender, but not browned – about 4 to 5 minutes. Add the garlic and air-fry for another minute. Transfer the onion and garlic to a mixing bowl and add the ground lamb, parsley, oregano, olives, feta cheese, salt and pepper. Gently mix the ingredients together.

2. Divide the mixture into 3 or 4 equal portions and then form the hamburgers, being careful not to over-handle the meat. One good way to do this is to throw the meat back and forth between your hands like a baseball, packing the meat each time you catch it. Flatten the balls into patties, making an indentation in the center of each patty. Flatten the sides of the patties as well to make it easier to fit them into the air fryer oven.

3. Preheat the toaster oven to 370°F.

4. If you don't have room for all four burgers, air-fry two or three burgers at a time for 8 minutes at 370°F. Flip the burgers over and air-fry for another 8 minutes. If you cooked your burgers in batches, return the first batch of burgers to the air fryer oven for the last two minutes of cooking to re-heat. This should give you a medium-well burger. If you'd prefer a medium-rare burger, shorten the cooking time to about 13 minutes. Remove the burgers to a resting plate and let the burgers rest for a few minutes before dressing and serving.

5. While the burgers are resting, toast the pita breads in the air fryer oven for 2 minutes. Tuck the burgers into the toasted pita breads, or wrap the pitas around the burgers and serve with a tzatziki sauce or some mayonnaise.

Steak Pinwheels With Pepper Slaw And Minneapolis Potato Salad

Servings: 4

Cooking Time: 16 Minutes

Ingredients:

- ➢ Brushing mixture:
- ➢ ½ cup cold strong brewed coffee
- ➢ 2 tablespoons molasses
- ➢ 1 tablespoon tomato paste
- ➢ 2 garlic cloves, minced
- ➢ 1 tablespoon olive oil
- ➢ Garlic powder
- ➢ 1 teaspoon butcher's pepper
- ➢ 1 pound lean, boneless beefsteak, flattened to ⅛-inch thickness with a meat mallet or rolling pin (place steak between 2 sheets of heavy-duty plastic wrap)

Directions:

1. Combine the brushing mixture ingredients in a small bowl and set aside.

2. Cut the steak into 2 × 3-inch strips, brush with the mixture, and roll up, securing the edges with toothpicks. Brush again with the mixture and place in an oiled or nonstick 8½ × 8½ × 2-inch square baking (cake) pan.

3. BROIL for 8 minutes, then turn with tongs, brush with the mixture again, and broil for another 8 minutes, or until browned.

Beef Vegetable Stew

Servings: 4

Cooking Time: 120 Minutes

Ingredients:

- 1 pound lean stewing beef, cut into 1-inch chunks
- 2 carrots, diced
- 2 celery stalks
- 1 large potato, diced
- ½ sweet onion, chopped
- 2 teaspoons minced garlic
- 1 (15-ounce) can diced tomatoes, with juices
- 1 teaspoon sea salt
- ½ teaspoon freshly ground black pepper
- 1 cup low-sodium beef broth
- 3 tablespoons all-purpose flour
- 1 cup frozen peas

Directions:

1. Place the rack in position 1 and preheat the toaster oven to 375°F on BAKE for 5 minutes.

2. In a 1½-quart casserole dish, combine the beef, carrots, celery, potato, onion, garlic, tomatoes, salt, and pepper.

3. In a small bowl, stir the broth and flour until well combined. Add the broth mixture to the beef mixture and stir to combine.

4. Cover with foil or a lid and bake for 2 hours, stirring each time you reset the timer, until the meat is very tender.

5. Stir in the peas and let stand for 10 minutes. Serve.

VEGETABLES AND VEGETARIAN

Ratatouille

Servings: 4

Cooking Time: 60 Minutes

Ingredients:

- ➢ Oil spray (hand-pumped)
- ➢ 1 eggplant, peeled and diced into ½-inch chunks
- ➢ 2 tomatoes, diced
- ➢ 1 zucchini, diced
- ➢ 2 bell peppers (any color), diced
- ➢ ½ red onion, chopped
- ➢ ½ cup tomato paste
- ➢ 2 teaspoons minced garlic
- ➢ 1 teaspoon dried basil
- ➢ ¼ teaspoon sea salt
- ➢ ⅛ teaspoon freshly ground black pepper
- ➢ Pinch red pepper flakes
- ➢ ½ cup low-sodium vegetable broth

Directions:

1. Place the rack in position 1 and preheat oven to 350°F on CONVECTION BAKE for 5 minutes.

2. Lightly coat a 1½-quart casserole dish with oil spray.

3. In a large bowl, toss the eggplant, tomatoes, zucchini, bell peppers, onion, tomato paste, garlic, basil, salt, black pepper, and red pepper flakes until well combined.

4. Transfer the vegetable mixture to the casserole dish, pour in the vegetable broth, and cover tightly with foil or a lid.

5. Convection bake for 1 hour, stirring once at the halfway mark, until the vegetables are very tender. Serve.

Classic Baked Potatoes

Servings: 4

Cooking Time: 50 Minutes

Ingredients:

- ➢ 4 medium baking potatoes,
- ➢ scrubbed and pierced with a fork

Directions:

1. Preheat the toaster oven to 450° F.
2. BAKE the potatoes on the oven rack for 50 minutes, or until tender when pierced with a fork.

Homemade Potato Puffs

Servings: 4

Cooking Time: 15 Minutes

Ingredients:

- 1¾ cups Water
- 4 tablespoons (¼ cup/½ stick) Butter
- 2 cups plus 2 tablespoons Instant mashed potato flakes
- 1½ teaspoons Table salt
- ¾ teaspoon Ground black pepper
- ¼ teaspoon Mild paprika
- ¼ teaspoon Dried thyme
- 1¼ cups Seasoned Italian-style dried bread crumbs (gluten-free, if a concern)
- Olive oil spray

Directions:

1. Heat the water with the butter in a medium saucepan set over medium-low heat just until the butter melts. Do not bring to a boil.

2. Remove the saucepan from the heat and stir in the potato flakes, salt, pepper, paprika, and thyme until smooth. Set aside to cool for 5 minutes.

3. Preheat the toaster oven to 400°F. Spread the bread crumbs on a dinner plate.

4. Scrape up 2 tablespoons of the potato flake mixture and form it into a small, oblong puff, like a little cylinder about 1½ inches long. Gently roll the puff in the bread crumbs until coated on all sides. Set it aside and continue making more, about 12 for the small batch, 18 for the medium batch, or 24 for the large.

5. Coat the potato cylinders with olive oil spray on all sides, then arrange them in the air fryer oven in one layer with some air space between them. Air-fry undisturbed for 15 minutes, or until crisp and brown.

6. Gently dump the contents of the air fryer oven onto a wire rack. Cool for 5 minutes before serving.

Mashed Potato Tots

Servings: 18

Cooking Time: 10 Minutes

Ingredients:

- ➤ 1 medium potato or 1 cup cooked mashed potatoes
- ➤ 1 tablespoon real bacon bits
- ➤ 2 tablespoons chopped green onions, tops only
- ➤ ¼ teaspoon onion powder
- ➤ 1 teaspoon dried chopped chives
- ➤ salt
- ➤ 2 tablespoons flour
- ➤ 1 egg white, beaten
- ➤ ½ cup panko breadcrumbs
- ➤ oil for misting or cooking spray

Directions:

1. If using cooked mashed potatoes, jump to step 4.

2. Peel potato and cut into ½-inch cubes. (Small pieces cook more quickly.) Place in saucepan, add water to cover, and heat to boil. Lower heat slightly and continue cooking just until tender, about 10 minutes.

3. Drain potatoes and place in ice cold water. Allow to cool for a minute or two, then drain well and mash.

4. Preheat the toaster oven to 390°F.

5. In a large bowl, mix together the potatoes, bacon bits, onions, onion powder, chives, salt to taste, and flour. Add egg white and stir well.

6. Place panko crumbs on a sheet of wax paper.

7. For each tot, use about 2 teaspoons of potato mixture. To shape, drop the measure of potato mixture onto panko crumbs and push crumbs up and around potatoes to coat edges. Then turn tot over to coat other side with crumbs.

8. Mist tots with oil or cooking spray and place in air fryer oven, crowded but not stacked.

9. Air-fry at 390°F for 10 minutes, until browned and crispy.

10. Repeat steps 8 and 9 to cook remaining tots.

Home Fries

Servings: 4

Cooking Time: 20 Minutes

Ingredients:

- ➤ 3 pounds potatoes, cut into 1-inch cubes
- ➤ ½ teaspoon oil
- ➤ salt and pepper

Directions:

1. In a large bowl, mix the potatoes and oil thoroughly.
2. Air-fry at 390°F for 10 minutes and redistribute potatoes.
3. Air-fry for an additional 10 minutes, until brown and crisp.
4. Season with salt and pepper to taste.

Sesame Carrots And Sugar Snap Peas

Servings: 16

Cooking Time: 4 Minutes

Ingredients:

- 1 pound carrots, peeled sliced on the bias (½-inch slices)
- 1 teaspoon olive oil
- salt and freshly ground black pepper
- ⅓ cup honey
- 1 tablespoon sesame oil
- 1 tablespoon soy sauce
- ½ teaspoon minced fresh ginger
- 4 ounces sugar snap peas (about 1 cup)
- 1½ teaspoons sesame seeds

Directions:

1. Preheat the toaster oven to 360°F.
2. Toss the carrots with the olive oil, season with salt and pepper and air-fry for 10 minutes.
3. Combine the honey, sesame oil, soy sauce and minced ginger in a large bowl. Add the sugar snap peas and the air-fried carrots to the honey mixture, toss to coat and return everything to the air fryer oven.
4. Turn up the temperature to 400°F and air-fry for an additional 6 minutes.
5. Transfer the carrots and sugar snap peas to a serving bowl. Pour the sauce from the bottom of the cooker over the vegetables and sprinkle sesame seeds over top. Serve immediately.

Rolled Chinese (napa) Cabbage With Chickpea Filling

Servings: 4

Cooking Time: 46 Minutes

Ingredients:

- 6 Chinese cabbage leaves, approximately 7 inches long
- Filling:
- 2 tablespoons low-fat ricotta cheese or Yogurt Cheese Spread
- 1 cup canned chickpeas (garbanzos), drained and mashed
- 1 teaspoon lemon juice
- Salt and butcher's pepper to taste
- 2 tablespoons olive oil for brushing
- 2 tablespoons chopped almonds

Directions:

1. Layer an 8½ × 8½ × 2-inch square baking (cake) pan with the cabbage leaves and add enough water to barely cover them.

2. BROIL 5 minutes, turn the leaves with tongs, and broil another 5 minutes, or until the leaves are partially cooked and just pliable. Spread the leaves on paper towels to drain and cool.

3. Mix the filling ingredients together in a medium bowl and adjust the seasonings to taste. Place equal portions of filling 2 inches from the stem end (base of the leaf) and roll up the leaf, enclosing the filling. Place each roll with the leaf edge down in an oiled or 8½ × 8½ × 2-inch square baking (cake) pan. Sprinkle with the almonds. Cover the pan with aluminum foil.

4. BAKE at 400° F. for 30 minutes, or until the rolls are tender. Remove the cover.

5. BROIL 6 minutes, or until the almonds and cabbage leaves are lightly browned.

Classic Stuffed Baked Potatoes

Servings: 4

Cooking Time: 58 Minutes

Ingredients:

- ➢ 2 large baking potatoes, slit on top with a knife
- ➢ ⅛ teaspoon paprika
- ➢ Salt and freshly ground black pepper to taste
- ➢ Stuffing:
- ➢ 1 teaspoon margarine
- ➢ 1 egg, lightly beaten
- ➢ ½ cup nonfat sour cream
- ➢ 4 tablespoons fresh or frozen and thawed chives

Directions:

1. Preheat the toaster oven to 400° F.

2. BAKE the potatoes on the oven rack for 50 minutes, or until tender. Open the slits with a knife and scoop out the pulp with a teaspoon. Set the potato shells aside.

3. Combine the stuffing ingredients and add the pulp, mixing well, until light and fluffy. Refill the potato shells.

4. BROIL 8 minutes, or until the top is lightly browned. Sprinkle with the chives before serving.

Classic Falafel

Servings: 4

Cooking Time: 14 Minutes

Ingredients:

- 1 (15-ounce) can low-sodium chickpeas, drained and rinsed
- 3 shallots, roughly chopped
- 3 tablespoons chickpea flour
- ¼ cup fresh parsley, roughly chopped
- 2 tablespoons cilantro, chopped
- 2 teaspoons minced garlic
- 1 teaspoon ground coriander
- 1 teaspoon ground cumin
- ½ teaspoon sea salt
- ⅛ teaspoon allspice
- Oil spray (hand-pumped)

Directions:

1. Preheat the toaster oven to 350°F on AIR FRY for 5 minutes.
2. Place the chickpeas in a food processor and pulse until roughly chopped.
3. Add the shallots, flour, parsley, cilantro, garlic, coriander, cumin, salt, and allspice, and pulse to form a thick paste.
4. Roll the chickpea mixture into 2-inch balls and flatten them slightly with the palm of your hand.
5. Place the air-fryer basket in the baking tray and coat it generously with oil spray.
6. Place the falafel in a single layer in the basket. Spray the patties with oil on both sides. You might have to work in batches.
7. Place the tray in position 2 and air fry until golden, turning halfway through, for about 14 minutes in total. Repeat with remaining patties. Serve.

Rosemary New Potatoes

Servings: 4

Cooking Time: 6 Minutes

Ingredients:

- ➢ 3 large red potatoes (enough to make 3 cups sliced)
- ➢ ¼ teaspoon ground rosemary
- ➢ ¼ teaspoon ground thyme
- ➢ ⅛ teaspoon salt
- ➢ ⅛ teaspoon ground black pepper
- ➢ 2 teaspoons extra-light olive oil

Directions:

1. Preheat the toaster oven to 330°F.
2. Place potatoes in large bowl and sprinkle with rosemary, thyme, salt, and pepper.
3. Stir with a spoon to distribute seasonings evenly.
4. Add oil to potatoes and stir again to coat well.
5. Air-fry at 330°F for 4 minutes. Stir and break apart any that have stuck together.
6. Cook an additional 2 minutes or until fork-tender.

Roasted Garlic

Servings: 1

Cooking Time: 20 Minutes

Ingredients:

- ➢ 3 whole garlic buds
- ➢ 3 tablespoons olive oil
- ➢ Salt and freshly ground black pepper

Directions:

1. Preheat the toaster oven to 450° F.

2. Place the garlic buds in an oiled or nonstick 8½ × 8½ × 2-inch square baking (cake) pan.

3. BAKE, uncovered, for 20 minutes, or until the buds are tender when pierced with a skewer or sharp knife. When cool enough to handle, peel and mash the baked cloves with a fork into the olive oil. Season with salt and pepper to taste.

Crispy Herbed Potatoes

Servings: 6

Cooking Time: 20 Minutes

Ingredients:

- 3 medium baking potatoes, washed and cubed
- ½ teaspoon dried thyme
- 1 teaspoon minced dried rosemary
- ½ teaspoon garlic powder
- 1 teaspoon sea salt
- ½ teaspoon black pepper
- 2 tablespoons extra-virgin olive oil
- ¼ cup chopped parsley

Directions:

1. Preheat the toaster oven to 390°F.
2. Pat the potatoes dry. In a large bowl, mix together the cubed potatoes, thyme, rosemary, garlic powder, sea salt, and pepper. Drizzle and toss with olive oil.
3. Pour the herbed potatoes into the air fryer oven. Air-fry for 20 minutes, stirring every 5 minutes.
4. Toss the cooked potatoes with chopped parsley and serve immediately.
5. VARY IT! Potatoes are versatile — add any spice or seasoning mixture you prefer and create your own favorite side dish.

LUNCH AND DINNER

Couscous-stuffed Poblano Peppers

Servings: 6

Cooking Time: 35 Minutes

Ingredients:

- 2 tablespoons olive oil
- ⅔ cup Israeli couscous
- 1 ¼ cups vegetable broth or water
- Kosher salt and freshly ground black pepper
- ½ medium onion, chopped
- 2 cloves garlic, minced
- 1 teaspoon dried oregano leaves
- ½ teaspoon ground cumin
- 1 (14.5-ounce) can fire-roasted diced tomatoes, with liquid
- Nonstick cooking spray
- 3 large poblano peppers, halved lengthwise, seeds and stem removed
- 1 ½ cups shredded Mexican blend, pepper Jack, or sharp cheddar cheese
- Optional toppings: minced fresh cilantro, sliced jalapeño peppers, diced tomatoes, sliced green onions (white and green portions)

Directions:

1. Heat 1 tablespoon oil in a medium saucepan over medium heat. Add the couscous and cook, stirring frequently, until golden brown, 2 to 3 minutes. Stir in the broth and season with salt and pepper. Cover, reduce the heat to a simmer, and cook, stirring occasionally, for about 10 minutes or until the liquid is absorbed. Remove from the heat and let stand, covered, for 5 minutes. Remove the cover, stir, and set aside to cool.

2. Heat the remaining 1 tablespoon oil in a small saucepan over medium heat. Add the onion, and cook, stirring frequently, for 3 to 5 minutes or until tender. Stir in the garlic and cook for 30 seconds. Stir in the oregano and cumin and season with salt and pepper. Stir in the tomatoes and simmer for 5 minutes.

3. Preheat the toaster oven to 400°F. Spray a 9-inch square baking pan with nonstick cooking spray. Spoon about one-third of the tomato mixture into the prepared pan. Arrange the peppers, cut side up, in the pan.

4. Stir 1 cup of the cheese into the couscous. Spoon the couscous mixture into the peppers, mounding slightly. Spoon the remaining tomato mixture over the peppers. Cover the pan and bake for 30 minutes.

5. Uncover the pan and sprinkle with the remaining cheese. Bake for 5 minutes or until the cheese is melted.

6. Top as desired with any of the various topping choices.

Light Beef Stroganoff

Servings: 4

Cooking Time: 40 Minutes

Ingredients:

- Sauce:
- 1 cup skim milk
- 1 cup fat-free half-and-half
- 2 tablespoons reduced-fat cream cheese, at room temperature
- 4 tablespoons unbleached flour
- 2 pounds lean round or sirloin steak, cut into strips 2 inches long and ½ inch thick
- Browning mixture:
- 1 tablespoon soy sauce
- 2 tablespoons spicy brown mustard
- 1 tablespoon olive oil
- 2 teaspoons garlic powder
- Salt and freshly ground black pepper to taste

Directions:

1. Whisk together the sauce ingredients in a medium bowl until smooth. Set aside.

2. Combine the beef strips and browning mixture ingredients in an oiled or nonstick 8½ × 8½ × 2-inch square baking (cake) pan.

3. BROIL for 8 minutes, or until the strips are browned, turning with tongs after 4 minutes. Transfer to a 1-quart 8½ × 8½ × 4-inch ovenproof baking dish. Add the sauce and mix well. Adjust the seasonings to taste. Cover with aluminum foil.

4. BAKE, covered, for 40 minutes, or until the meat is tender.

Nice + Easy Baked Macaroni + Cheese

Servings: 6

Cooking Time: 35 Minutes

Ingredients:

- Nonstick cooking spray
- 2 cups whole milk
- 3 ounces cream cheese
- ½ teaspoon kosher salt
- 1 clove garlic
- ¼ teaspoon freshly ground black pepper
- 8 ounces macaroni, uncooked
- 2 cups shredded cheddar cheese
- 2 tablespoons unsalted butter, melted
- ¼ cup grated Parmesan cheese
- 1 cup panko bread crumbs

Directions:

1. Preheat the toaster oven to 425°F. Spray an 11 x 7 x 2 ½-inch baking dish with nonstick cooking spray.

2. Place the milk, cream cheese, salt, garlic, and pepper into a blender. Blend until smooth.

3. Add macaroni to the prepared dish. Sprinkle with the cheddar cheese. Pour the milk mixture over all.

4. Combine the butter, Parmesan, and panko in a small bowl. Sprinkle the crumb mixture over the macaroni. Bake, uncovered, for 25 to 35 minutes or until the top is golden brown. Remove from the oven and let stand for at least 10 minutes.

Spanako Pizza

Servings: 2

Cooking Time: 30 Minutes

Ingredients:

- 8 sheets phyllo dough, thawed and folded in half
- 4 tablespoons olive oil
- 4 tablespoons grated Parmesan cheese
- Topping mixture:
- 1 10-ounce package frozen chopped spinach, thawed and well drained
- 1 plum tomato, finely chopped
- ¼ cup finely chopped onion
- ¼ cup shredded low-fat mozzarella cheese
- 3 tablespoons crumbled feta cheese or part-skim ricotta cheese
- 2 garlic cloves, minced
- Salt and freshly ground black pepper to taste

Directions:

1. Preheat the toaster oven to 375° F.

2. Layer the sheets of phyllo dough in an oiled or nonstick 9¾-inch-diameter baking pan, lightly brushing the top of each sheet with olive oil and folding in the corner edges to fit the pan.

3. Combine the topping mixture ingredients in a bowl and adjust the seasonings to taste. Spread the mixture on top of the phyllo pastry layers and sprinkle with the Parmesan cheese.

4. BAKE for 30 minutes, or until the cheese is melted and the topping is lightly browned. Remove carefully from the pan with a metal spatula.

Crab Chowder

Servings: 4

Cooking Time: 40 Minutes

Ingredients:

- 1 6-ounce can lump crabmeat, drained and chopped, or ½ pound fresh crabmeat, cleaned and chopped
- 1 cup skim milk or low-fat soy milk
- 1 cup fat-free half-and-half
- 2 tablespoons unbleached flour
- ¼ cup chopped onion
- ½ cup peeled and diced potato
- 1 carrot, peeled and chopped
- 1 celery stalk, chopped
- 2 garlic cloves, minced
- 2 tablespoons chopped fresh parsley
- ½ teaspoon ground cumin
- 1 teaspoon paprika
- Salt and butcher's pepper to taste

Directions:

1. Preheat the toaster oven to 400° F.

2. Whisk together the milk, half-and-half, and flour in a bowl. Transfer the mixture to a 1-quart 8½ × 8½ × 4-inch ovenproof baking dish. Add all the other ingredients, mixing well. Adjust the seasonings to taste.

3. BAKE, covered, for 40 minutes, or until the vegetables are tender.

Chicken Tortilla Roll-ups

Servings: 4

Cooking Time: 10 Minutes

Ingredients:

- Nonstick cooking spray
- ¼ cup olive oil
- 2 cloves garlic, minced
- 1 ½ cups shredded cooked chicken
- 1 cup shredded Mexican blend or cheddar cheese
- ½ cup frozen corn, thawed
- ⅓ cup salsa verde
- 1 green onion, white and green portions, chopped
- 2 tablespoons minced fresh cilantro
- 1 tablespoon fresh lime juice
- ½ teaspoon ground cumin
- ¼ teaspoon Sriracha or hot sauce
- Kosher salt and freshly ground black pepper
- 8 flour tortillas, about 8 inches in diameter
- Optional toppings: minced cilantro, salsa, guacamole, sour cream

Directions:

1. Preheat the toaster oven to 375°F. Spray a 12 x 12-inch baking pan with nonstick cooking spray.

2. Stir the oil and garlic in a small bowl; set aside.

3. Stir the chicken, cheese, corn, salsa verde, green onion, cilantro, lime juice, cumin, and Sriracha in a large bowl. Season with salt and pepper.

4. Brush both sides of a tortilla very lightly with the garlic oil. Spoon about ⅓ cup chicken filling on the lower side of the tortilla. Roll the tortilla over the filling. Place the filled tortilla, seam side down, in the prepared baking pan. Repeat with the remaining tortillas and filling.

5. Brush the tops of each filled tortilla with the remaining garlic oil, coating them evenly and especially covering the edges of the tortillas.

6. Bake, uncovered, for 10 minutes or until the tortillas are crisp and the filling is hot. Serve with your choice of any of the various toppings.

Fresh Herb Veggie Pizza

Servings: 4

Cooking Time: 25 Minutes

Ingredients:

- 1 9-inch ready-made pizza crust
- 1 tablespoon olive oil
- 1 4-ounce can tomato paste
- 2 tablespoons shredded part-skim mozzarella
- 2 tablespoons grated Parmesan cheese
- 2 tablespoons crumbled feta cheese
- ½ bell pepper, chopped
- 1 tablespoon chopped fresh parsley
- 1 tablespoon chopped fresh oregano
- 1 tablespoon chopped fresh basil
- ½ teaspoon red pepper flakes
- Salt and freshly ground black pepper to taste
- Pizza mixture:
- 2 garlic cloves, minced
- 1 plum tomato, chopped

Directions:

1. Preheat the toaster oven to 400° F.
2. Brush the pizza crust with olive oil and spread the tomato paste evenly to cover.
3. Combine the ingredients for the pizza mixture and spread evenly on top of the tomato paste layer. Sprinkle the cheeses over all and season to taste. Place the pizza on the toaster oven rack.
4. BAKE for 25 minutes, or until the vegetables are cooked and the cheese is melted.

Honey Bourbon–glazed Pork Chops With Sweet Potatoes + Apples

Servings: 2

Cooking Time: 42 Minutes

Ingredients:

- Nonstick cooking spray
- 2 medium sweet potatoes, peeled and quartered
- 2 tablespoons bourbon
- 2 tablespoons honey
- 1 tablespoon canola or vegetable oil
- ½ teaspoon onion powder
- ½ teaspoon dry mustard
- ¼ teaspoon dried thyme leaves
- Kosher salt and freshly ground black pepper
- 2 bone-in pork chops, cut about ¾ inch thick
- 1 Granny Smith apple, not peeled, cored and cut into ½-inch wedges

Directions:

1. Preheat the toaster oven to 375°F. Spray a 12 x 12-inch baking pan with nonstick cooking spray.

2. Place the sweet potatoes on one side of the prepared pan. Spray with nonstick cooking spray. Bake, uncovered, for 20 minutes.

3. Meanwhile, stir the bourbon, honey, oil, onion powder, mustard, and thyme in a small bowl. Season with salt and pepper and set aside.

4. Turn the potatoes over. Place the pork chops on the other end of the pan in a single layer. Arrange the apple wedges around the potatoes and pork chops, stacking the apples as needed. Brush the bourbon mixture generously over all. Bake for 15 to 18 minutes or until the pork is done as desired and a meat thermometer registers a minimum of 145°F.

5. For additional browning, set the toaster oven to Broil and broil for 2 to 4 minutes, or until the edges are brown as desired.

6. Transfer to a serving platter. Spoon any drippings over the meat and vegetables. Let stand for 5 minutes before serving.

Sheet Pan Loaded Nachos

Servings: 4

Cooking Time: 13 Minutes

Ingredients:

- 1 tablespoon canola or vegetable oil
- ½ pound lean ground beef
- ½ cup chopped onion
- 2 cloves garlic, minced
- 1 teaspoon chili powder
- ½ teaspoon ground cumin
- Kosher salt and freshly ground black pepper
- 6 ounces tortilla chips
- ½ cup canned black beans, rinsed and drained
- 1 ½ cups shredded sharp cheddar cheese or Mexican blend cheese
- ½ cup salsa
- Optional toppings: sliced jalapeño peppers, chopped bell peppers, sliced ripe olives, chopped tomatoes, minced fresh cilantro, sour cream, chopped avocado, guacamole, or chopped onion.

Directions:

1. Preheat the toaster oven to 400°F. Line a 12 x 12-inch baking pan with nonstick aluminum foil. (Or if lining the pan with regular foil, spray it with nonstick cooking spray.)

2. Heat the oil in a large skillet over medium-high heat. Add the ground beef and onion and cook, stirring frequently, until the beef is almost done. Add the garlic, chili powder, cumin, season with salt and pepper, and cook, stirring frequently, until the beef is fully cooked; drain.

3. Arrange the tortilla chips in an even layer in the prepared pan. Top with the beef-onion mixture, then top with the beans. Bake, uncovered, for 6 to 8 minutes. Top with the cheese and bake for 5 minutes more, or until the cheese is melted.

4. Drizzle with the salsa. Top as desired with any of the various toppings.

Italian Baked Stuffed Tomatoes

Servings: 4

Cooking Time: 30 Minutes

Ingredients:

- 4 large tomatoes
- 1 cup shredded chicken
- 1 1/2 cup shredded mozzarella, divided
- 1 1/2 cup cooked rice
- 2 tablespoon minced onion
- 1/4 cup grated parmesan cheese
- 1 tablespoon dried Italian seasoning
- salt
- pepper
- Basil

Directions:

1. Preheat the toaster oven to 350°F. Spray toaster oven pan with nonstick cooking spray.

2. Cut the top off each tomato and scoop centers out. Place bottoms on prepared pan. Chop 3 tomatoes (about 1 1/2 cup, chopped) and add to large bowl.

3. Add shredded chicken, 1 cup shredded mozzarella cheese, rice, onion, Parmesan cheese, Italian seasoning, salt and pepper to large bowl and stir until blended. Divide between tomatoes, about 1 cup per tomato. Top with remaining mozzarella and tomato top.

4. Bake 25 to 30 minutes until cheese is melted and mixture is heated through.

5. Garnish with basil before serving.

Middle Eastern Roasted Chicken

Servings: 4

Cooking Time: 25 Minutes

Ingredients:

- 3 tablespoons fresh lemon juice
- ¼ cup plus 1 tablespoon olive oil
- 4 cloves garlic, minced
- ½ teaspoon kosher salt
- 1 teaspoon freshly ground black pepper
- 1 teaspoon ground cumin
- 1 teaspoon paprika
- ½ teaspoon turmeric
- ⅛ teaspoon red pepper flakes
- 1 pound boneless, skinless chicken breasts
- 1 large onion, cut into thin wedges

Directions:

1. Whisk the lemon juice, ¼ cup olive oil, garlic, salt, pepper, cumin, paprika, turmeric, and red pepper flakes in a small bowl until blended.

2. Cut the chicken breast lengthwise into thin scaloppine slices. Place the chicken in a nonreactive dish and pour the marinade over the chicken. Turn the chicken to coat thoroughly and evenly. Cover, refrigerate, and marinate for at least 1 hour and up to 10 hours. (The longer the better, as the flavor melds with the chicken.)

3. Remove the chicken from the refrigerator and add the onion to the marinade.

4. Preheat the toaster oven to 425°F. Brush the remaining tablespoon of olive oil over the bottom of a 12 x 12-inch pan. Place the chicken pieces on one side of the baking sheet and the onion wedges on the other side in a single layer. Discard any remaining marinade.

5. Roast for 20 to 25 minutes or until the chicken is browned and a meat thermometer registers 165°F. Remove from the oven and let rest a few minutes, then slice the chicken into thin strips. Toss with the onion and serve.

Very Quick Pizza

Servings: 1

Cooking Time: 3 Minutes

Ingredients:

- ➢ 2 tablespoons salsa
- ➢ 1 6-inch whole wheat pita bread
- ➢ 2 tablespoons shredded part-skim, low-moisture mozzarella cheese

Directions:

1. Spread the salsa on the pita bread and sprinkle with the cheese.
2. TOAST once, or until the cheese is melted.

DESSERTS

Hasselback Apple Crisp

Servings: 4   Cooking Time: 20 Minutes

Ingredients:

- 2 large Gala apples, peeled, cored and cut in half
- ¼ cup butter, melted
- ½ teaspoon ground cinnamon
- 2 tablespoons sugar
- Topping
- 3 tablespoons butter, melted
- 2 tablespoons brown sugar
- ¼ cup chopped pecans
- 2 tablespoons rolled oats
- 1 tablespoon flour
- vanilla ice cream
- caramel sauce

Directions:

1. Place the apples cut side down on a cutting board. Slicing from stem end to blossom end, make 8 to 10 slits down the apple halves but only slice three quarters of the way through the apple, not all the way through to the cutting board.

2. Preheat the toaster oven to 330°F and pour a little water into the bottom of the air fryer oven drawer. (This will help prevent the grease that drips into the bottom drawer from burning and smoking.)

3. Transfer the apples to the air fryer oven, flat side down. Combine ¼ cup of melted butter, cinnamon and sugar in a small bowl. Brush this butter mixture onto the apples and air-fry at 330°F for 15 minutes. Baste the apples several times with the butter mixture during the cooking process.

4. While the apples are air-frying, make the filling. Combine 3 tablespoons of melted butter with the brown sugar, pecans, rolled oats and flour in a bowl. Stir with a fork until the mixture resembles small crumbles.

5. When the timer on the air fryer oven is up, spoon the topping down the center of the apples. Air-fry at 330°F for an additional 5 minutes.

6. Transfer the apples to a serving plate and serve with vanilla ice cream and caramel sauce.

Sweet Potato Donut Holes

Servings: 18

Cooking Time: 4 Minutes

Ingredients:

- 1 cup flour
- ⅓ cup sugar
- ¼ teaspoon baking soda
- 1 teaspoon baking powder
- ⅛ teaspoon salt
- ½ cup cooked mashed purple sweet potatoes
- 1 egg, beaten
- 2 tablespoons butter, melted
- 1 teaspoon pure vanilla extract
- oil for misting or cooking spray

Directions:

1. Preheat the toaster oven to 390°F.
2. In a large bowl, stir together the flour, sugar, baking soda, baking powder, and salt.
3. In a separate bowl, combine the potatoes, egg, butter, and vanilla and mix well.
4. Add potato mixture to dry ingredients and stir into a soft dough.
5. Shape dough into 1½-inch balls. Mist lightly with oil or cooking spray.
6. Place 9 donut holes in air fryer oven, leaving a little space in between. Air-fry for 4 minutes, until done in center and lightly browned outside.
7. Repeat step 6 to cook remaining donut holes.

Scones

Servings: 8

Cooking Time: 20 Minutes

Ingredients:

- ➢ Scone mixture:
- ➢ 1 cup unbleached flour
- ➢ 1 teaspoon baking powder
- ➢ 2 ¼ cup brown sugar
- ➢ 3 tablespoons vegetable oil
- ➢ 4 ¼ cup low-fat buttermilk
- ➢ 5 ½ teaspoon vanilla extract
- ➢ Topping mixture:
- ➢ 1 tablespoon granulated sugar
- ➢ 1 tablespoon margarine
- ➢ 1 teaspoon ground cinnamon

Directions:

1. Preheat the toaster oven to 425° F.

2. Combine the scone mixture ingredients in a medium bowl, cutting to blend with 2 butter knives or a pastry blender. Add a little more buttermilk, if necessary, so that the dough is moist enough to stay together when pinched.

3. KNEAD the dough on a lightly floured surface for 2 minutes, then place the dough in an oiled or nonstick 9¾-inch round cake pan and pat down to spread out evenly to the edges of the pan. Cut into 8 wedges.

4. Combine the topping mixture in a small bowl, mixing well, and sprinkle evenly on the dough.

5. BAKE for 20 minutes, or until golden brown.

Coconut Drop Cookies

Servings: 4

Cooking Time: 12 Minutes

Ingredients:

- 1 14-ounce package shredded and sweetened coconut
- 2 eggs
- 1 tablespoon margarine
- ¾ cup unbleached flour
- 1 teaspoon baking powder
- Salt to taste

Directions:

1. Preheat the toaster oven to 250° F.
2. Combine all the ingredients in a medium bowl, mixing well. Drop in small portions with a teaspoon onto an oiled or nonstick 6½ × 10-inch baking sheet or an oiled or nonstick 8½ × 8½ × 2-inch square baking (cake) pan.
3. BAKE for 10 minutes, or until golden brown.

Coconut Rice Cake

Servings: 8

Cooking Time: 30 Minutes

Ingredients:

- 1 cup all-natural coconut water
- 1 cup unsweetened coconut milk
- 1 teaspoon almond extract
- ¼ teaspoon salt
- 4 tablespoons honey
- cooking spray
- ¾ cup raw jasmine rice
- 2 cups sliced or cubed fruit

Directions:

1. In a medium bowl, mix together the coconut water, coconut milk, almond extract, salt, and honey.
2. Spray air fryer oven baking pan with cooking spray and add the rice.
3. Pour liquid mixture over rice.
4. Preheat the toaster oven to 360°F and air-fry for 15 minutes. Stir and air-fry for 15 minutes longer or until rice grains are tender.
5. Allow cake to cool slightly. Run a dull knife around edge of cake, inside the pan. Turn the cake out onto a platter and garnish with fruit.

Chewy Coconut Cake

Servings: 6

Cooking Time: 22 Minutes

Ingredients:

- ¾ cup plus 2½ tablespoons All-purpose flour
- ¾ teaspoon Baking powder
- ⅛ teaspoon Table salt
- 7½ tablespoons (1 stick minus ½ tablespoon) Butter, at room temperature
- ⅓ cup plus 1 tablespoon Granulated white sugar
- 5 tablespoons Packed light brown sugar
- 5 tablespoons Pasteurized egg substitute, such as Egg Beaters
- 2 teaspoons Vanilla extract
- ½ cup Unsweetened shredded coconut
- Baking spray

Directions:

1. Preheat the toaster oven to 325°F.

2. Mix the flour, baking powder, and salt in a small bowl until well combined.

3. Using an electric hand mixer at medium speed , beat the butter, granulated white sugar, and brown sugar in a medium bowl until creamy and smooth, about 3 minutes, occasionally scraping down the inside of the bowl. Beat in the egg substitute or egg and vanilla until smooth.

4. Scrape down and remove the beaters. Fold in the flour mixture with a rubber spatula just until all the flour is moistened. Fold in the coconut until the mixture is a uniform color.

5. Use the baking spray to generously coat the inside of a 6-inch round cake pan for a small batch, a 7-inch round cake pan for a medium batch, or an 8-inch round cake pan for a large batch. Scrape and spread the batter into the pan, smoothing the batter out to an even layer.

6. Set the pan in the toaster oven and air-fry for 18 minutes for a 6-inch layer, 20 minutes for a 7-inch layer, or 22 minutes for an 8-inch layer, or until the cake is well browned and set even if there's a little soft give right at the center. Start checking it at the 16-minute mark to know where you are.

7. Use hot pads or silicone baking mitts to transfer the cake pan to a wire rack. Cool for at least 1 hour or up to 4 hours. Use a nonstick-safe knife to slice the cake into wedges right in the pan, lifting them out one by one.

Midnight Nutella® Banana Sandwich

Servings: 2

Cooking Time: 8 Minutes

Ingredients:

- ➢ butter, softened
- ➢ 4 slices white bread
- ➢ ¼ cup chocolate hazelnut spread (Nutella®)
- ➢ 1 banana

Directions:

1. Preheat the toaster oven to 370°F.

2. Spread the softened butter on one side of all the slices of bread and place the slices buttered side down on the counter. Spread the chocolate hazelnut spread on the other side of the bread slices. Cut the banana in half and then slice each half into three slices lengthwise. Place the banana slices on two slices of bread and top with the remaining slices of bread (buttered side up) to make two sandwiches. Cut the sandwiches in half (triangles or rectangles) – this will help them all fit in the air fryer oven at once. Transfer the sandwiches to the air fryer oven.

3. Air-fry at 370°F for 5 minutes. Flip the sandwiches over and air-fry for another 2 to 3 minutes, or until the top bread slices are nicely browned. Pour yourself a glass of milk or a midnight nightcap while the sandwiches cool slightly and enjoy!

Blueberry Clafoutis

Servings: 6

Cooking Time: 35 Minutes

Ingredients:

- 2 tablespoons salted butter, melted, plus extra for greasing the baking dish
- ½ cup all-purpose flour, plus extra for dusting the baking dish
- 2 cups fresh blueberries
- 1 cup whole milk
- 3 large eggs
- ½ cup granulated sugar
- ¼ cup light brown sugar
- 2 teaspoons vanilla extract

Directions:

1. Place the rack in position 1 and preheat the toaster oven to 350°F on BAKE for 5 minutes.
2. Lightly grease and flour a 9-inch-square baking dish.
3. Spread the blueberries in the bottom of the baking dish.
4. In a large bowl, whisk the milk, eggs, sugar, brown sugar, butter, and vanilla until smooth.
5. Add the flour and whisk to combine.
6. Pour the batter into the baking dish and bake for 35 minutes or until light brown and a toothpick inserted into the center comes out clean. If the top starts to get too brown, cover the dish lightly with foil.
7. Cool for 10 minutes and serve.

Raspberry Hand Pies

Servings: 6

Cooking Time: 20 Minutes

Ingredients:

- ➤ 2 cups fresh raspberries
- ➤ ¼ cup granulated sugar, plus extra for topping
- ➤ 1 tablespoon cornstarch
- ➤ 1 tablespoon freshly squeezed lemon juice
- ➤ 2 store-bought unbaked pie crusts
- ➤ 1 large egg
- ➤ 1 tablespoon water
- ➤ Oil spray (hand-pumped)

Directions:

1. Preheat the toaster oven to 350°F on AIR FRY for 5 minutes.
2. Place the air-fryer basket in the baking tray.
3. In a medium bowl, stir the raspberries, sugar, cornstarch, and lemon juice until well mixed.
4. Lay the pie crusts on a clean work surface and cut out 6 (6-inch) circles.
5. Evenly divide the raspberry mixture among the circles, placing it in the center.
6. In a small bowl, beat together the egg and water with a fork. Use the egg wash to lightly moisten the edges of the circles, then fold them over to create a half-moon shape. Use a fork to crimp around the rounded part of the pies to seal.
7. Lightly spray the pies with the oil and sprinkle with sugar. Cut 2 to 3 small slits in each pie and place three pies in the basket.
8. In position 2, air fry for 10 minutes until golden brown. Repeat with the remaining pies.
9. Cool the pies and serve.

Fried Snickers Bars

Servings: 8

Cooking Time: 4 Minutes

Ingredients:

- ⅓ cup All-purpose flour
- 1 Large egg white(s), beaten until foamy
- 1½ cups (6 ounces) Vanilla wafer cookie crumbs
- 8 Fun-size (0.6-ounce/17-gram) Snickers bars, frozen
- Vegetable oil spray

Directions:

1. Preheat the toaster oven to 400°F.

2. Set up and fill three shallow soup plates or small pie plates on your counter: one for the flour, one for the beaten egg white(s), and one for the cookie crumbs.

3. Unwrap the frozen candy bars. Dip one in the flour, turning it to coat on all sides. Gently stir any excess, then set it in the beaten egg white(s). Turn it to coat all sides, even the ends, then let any excess egg white slip back into the rest. Set the candy bar in the cookie crumbs. Turn to coat on all sides, even the ends. Dip the candy bar back in the egg white(s) a second time, then into the cookie crumbs a second time, making sure you have an even coating all around. Coat the covered candy bar all over with vegetable oil spray. Set aside so you can dip and coat the remaining candy bars.

4. Set the coated candy bars in the pan with as much air space between them as possible. Air-fry undisturbed for 4 minutes, or until golden brown.

5. Remove the pan from the machine and let the candy bars cool in the pan for 10 minutes. Use a nonstick-safe spatula to transfer them to a wire rack and cool for 5 minutes more before chowing down.